Some Scripture quotations are taken from the Holy Bible, New International Version®, NIV®. Copyright ©1973, 1978, 1984, 2011 by Biblica, Inc.™ Used by permission of Zondervan; Other Scripture quotations from THE MESSAGE. Copyright © by Eugene H. Peterson1993, 1994, 1995, 1996, 2000, 2001, 2002. Used by permission of Tyndale House Publishers, Inc.; Other Scripture quotations from The Holy Bible, English Standard Version® (ESV®)Copyright © 2001 by Crossway, a publishing ministry of Good News Publishers. Other Scripture quotations marked HCSB®, are taken from the Holman Christian Standard Bible®, Copyright © 1999, 2000, 2002, 2003, 2009 by Holman Bible Publishers. Used by permission. HCSB® is a federally registered trademark of Holman Bible Publishers.

All rights reserved.

Copyright © 2020 by Dale Davis
All Rights Reserved
ISBN-13:9798653556869
ISBN-13:9798653556869 (ebook)

"When God Seems To Hide"

The Esther Story

Dale Davis

Acknowledgments

I would like to thank Linwood Prince. A good friend who continually encourages me each day. I would like to thank Denise Luddeke. A good friend who continually encourages me to keep writing. I am grateful for their support, encouragement and prayers.

Table of Contents

Introduction

Chapter 1 - Impeached - Esther 1

Chapter 2 - Elected- Esther 2

Chapter 3 - Hated - Esther 3

Chapter 4 - Challenged - Esther 4

Chapter 5 - Exhilarated - Esther 5

Chapter 6 - Humiliated - Esther 6

Chapter 7 - Hanged - Esther 7

Chapter 8 - Countered - Esther 8

Chapter 9 - Slaughtered - Esther 9

Chapter 10 - Stately Genius - Esther 10

Conclusion

Summary and Interesting Facts

Introduction

A massive oak tree stood in the corner of the backyard where I grew up as a child. Between that tree and the longtime neighbor's fence was an extremely small space. That space had come to be one of my most favorite hiding places. When I was about nine or ten, I had gotten into trouble again, which was a daily occurrence with me. On this particular day, I ran out of the house, slamming the door in the process, ran across the backyard, taking a seat behind the oak tree. I was a very obstinate child, so I had decided I wasn't coming out of that place at all. This is a time when I didn't have a cell phone, so I wasn't spending time texting or looking at Facebook. Looking back on that day, I think I sit in that small corner for over five hours. I went out there about 6 p.m. I remember hearing my dad and my mom calling out my name, wondering where I was in the neighborhood. Nobody knew I liked to hide there, so they never came and looked behind that tree. I remember seeing police cars cruising the streets, I knew then they had called and reported I was missing. Finally, about 11 p.m., I came out of my hiding place, proud that I had stayed out there so long. When I shouted, "Here I am!", needless to say, my mother and father weren't too pleased with what I had done. I'm reasonably certain you can guess what came next.

I can recall my mom and dad calling my name over and over. I am certain they were worried, mad, and very frustrated because I would not answer them. How many times in my life have I encountered the same feeling when I call out to God and He seems hidden? At times, we may feel as though He is hiding behind a massive oak tree. How many times in your life have you experienced the same feeling? How often do we ponder why God is so distant?

One of the most underlying themes among Christians and non-Christians alike is that God seems hidden. Periodically it seems that God is somewhere out there in the darkness, hiding, but we don't know where.

Different things enter into our lives. We lose our job; we suffer from an excruciating illness, we feel the sting of a relationship gone awry, disappointments fall at our doorstep, leaving us wondering where God is. We pray, plead, beg, and ask, yet we find silence. We look to the sky, throw up our hands, calling for Him to come out of hiding, but still complete silence. There are times when cancer invades our lives, we encounter severe difficulties, or a loved one slips from this life, we assume God is far away.

Woven through the pages of God's Word, we see the undeniable actions of God. We recognize His greatness over and over. He delivers His people from the plight of the Egyptians; He speaks to Moses from a burning bush, He parts the Red Sea. Some hear His voice, others watch as the walls of Jericho crumble. In the New Testament, we watch as Jesus performs miracles, healing the blind, casting out demons, making the lame walk, or feeding a multitude. We sit on our couch, reading these events, we long for a miracle like these, we yearn to hear our name called. We stand to our feet shouting, "MY GOD IS REAL." But the next day as we drive to work, we do not hear God speak. We sit at our desk, the lone voice we hear is the voice of our boss. Devoting many hours to our jobs, we feel as if money controls our lives more than God does. When we arrive home, we turn on the television, staring at the screen, and wonder if God is real.

Every so often, life becomes a mess. Disasters strike, sickness invades, disappointments occupy our thinking, and dishonesty is all around us. We stand in

our kitchen, staring out the window, pondering why this loving, gracious, kind God is nowhere to be found. Then the "why" questions ravage our minds.
"Why did my son die on the way home from college?"
"Why can't I find a job?"
"Why did my mom have to succumb to cancer?"
"Why have my children left their Christian faith?"
"Why doesn't God heal my sickness?"
"Why did my parents get a divorce?"

When God seems hidden, these are the questions that arise. When we call His name and He doesn't seem to answer, these question entertain our thinking. I have been there, I have experienced this more times than I am willing to admit. I also know there are many others who have experienced these similar feelings. I have friends, co-workers, family members, who are disappointed with God. They are broken, disheartened, also wondering if God has gone on vacation. They are baffled with God, trying to figure out why He doesn't answer their prayers with bells and whistles, with signs and wonders, and dynamic miracles, as He did in the Bible.

If you are feeling this way, you are not alone. If you are in a constant state of turmoil, you are not alone. If God seems hidden to you, often, that kind of thinking is hard to rule out. You wish, you hope, you want God to come out of hiding. Therefore, I invite you to stroll down the streets of Persia with me, walk through the palace, roam in the garden, and look at the story of Esther. A place, a time, where God seemed distant, hidden, out of sight. A story where God's name is never mentioned once, where they didn't hear His voice and it seemed no miracles were performed.

I have been invited by the king to come and visit the palace and the city. He knows I am a writer, so he has sent me an invitation to a large party. He wants me to write a story about him. The invitation states that I am allowed to bring someone else along. Therefore, I am inviting you. Are you willing to go? I know I am.

Chapter 1 - "Impeachment"
Esther 1

PARTY TIME WITH THE KING-BANQUET #1 AND #2

Arriving in the capital city of Susa, I step off of the bus, and immediately I notice dignitaries, nobles, and military leaders making their way to the king's palace. With my invitation in hand, I follow those who are headed that way. I have my credentials with me as I walk to the gate that leads to the magnificent looking palace. The guard at the gate gives me a fierce look, obviously, he can tell I am not from around there. I show him my invitation. I say, "The king has invited me to write a story about him."

"So you are a scribe?" he asks.

"Yes, I am."

"Alright, go on in!"

I make my way down the pathway to the palace. I am escorted in by a young man. I am led down a long hallway. Many guests are arriving simultaneously. We soon arrive at a large banquet room. The beauty all around me is superb. The room is lined with tables constructed of marble, the chairs are made of gold and silver. At the head of these tables, I recognize the king in all his splendor. A royal crown upon his head. It is clearly apparent that each one in attendance knows who King Ahasuerus is. He is also known as King Xerxes. King Ahasuerus (Xerxes) is liked by all people. He is extremely favored. He sees me come in, motions for me to walk towards him. As I walk to the end of the long table, he says, "I am so delighted you were able to make it. I am very excited that you are here to write a story about me."

"I'm am very glad to be here. I want to thank you for the invitation."

After jotting a few things down, I find a seat at one of the tables. I hear whispers from a few people who are telling stories of how powerful, rich, and arrogant, King Ahasuerus is. One fellow leans over to me and says, "Those three words are his top three attributes." I make sure to put those words in my notes. As I am writing, the king stands up to speak, he says, "As most of you know, I am ruler over 127 provinces from India to Ethiopia. Welcome to my party."

Music begins playing. I look over to the far corner observing a group of musicians. All the various guests start talking. Before any food is served, I walk over to a fellow by the name of Memucan. I ask him, "How well do you know the king?"

He answers promptly, saying, "I've known him for a long time, I am one of his top counselors."

"Really! Do you think you would have a few minutes to tell me a little about him?" I question.

"No problem," he says. "But first, who are you?"

"I am a writer, and I am writing a story about the king."

"Oh, yeah, I should have known. The king told me you were coming."

"The story will be published in a book."

Memucan says, "I will tell you anything you desire to know, as long as I am mentioned in this, um, book."

"No problem!" I say.

Memucan sits down in a chair next to me and starts telling me about how the king has spent the last two years building this great kingdom. He informs me that King Ahasuerus is one of the most illustrious monarchs the world has ever known. Then with a stern face, he says, "Yeah, he has invited all these military leaders here because he is wanting to invade Greece.

King Ahasuerus is throwing this gala to see if he can sway them to consider this war."

After a few more questions and answers, Memucan is called away by some of his friends. As I am furiously writing some of the details down, I notice the food is being served, so I put my tablet away for awhile. One thing I am picking up on about this party is this is no ordinary party. Everyone is talking about how this party is going to last for 180 days. I think to myself, *"180 days, wow, what a party!"*

While I am eating, I watch as the king wanders through the crowd, shaking hands, pointing to unique aspects of the palace. I guess he is working really hard to impress all these guests. Not too long after our meal, we are placed into varied groups for a tour of the palace. I am automatically placed in the first group because they want to make sure nothing is left out of the book.

The king leads a group of military leaders, while the rest of us have one of his chief counselors as our tour guide. The first place we visit is the garden. Instantly, I am amazed by the fine drapes that hang from some enormous marble columns. At the top of these drapes are some silver rings, which attach the drape to the column. Tied around each drape are some linen cords made of white and purple material.

We leave the garden and move to a spacious room that contains couches made of gold and silver, just like the chairs in the banquet room. I look down, stunned by the beauty of the mosaic floor. Inset into this floor are pieces of marble, mother-of-pearl, sapphires, rubies, and diamonds. This floor must have cost a fortune. Some in the group decide to sit down on the golden couches.

As we head back to the banquet hall, I ask a few people what they thought of the palace. I heard words like, "impressive," "remarkable," and "extraordinary."

We make our way back to our original seats. As we are being seated, servants bring drinks to us. These drinks are served in cups made of gold. Each cup has a different design on it. Am I impressed? Absolutely, I am, how about you?

On the long bus ride, I had read a few books, the newspaper, and a magazine. Inside the pages of this magazine, an article captured my attention about the craziest things billionaires spend their money on. My attention was drawn to a small country in Asia called Brunei. *This country is smaller than the state of Deleware. The ruler, known as the Sultan of Brunei, is like King Ahasuerus. He is wealthy, but he has spent much of his wealth on cars. It is believed that he owns between 5,000 and 7,000 vehicles with a combined cost of about $5 billion. Among these rare cars are 21 Lamborghinis, 452 Ferraris, and 604 Rolls Royces. He also owns the world's most expensive car, called the "Star of India," a $14 million Rolls convertible.*

As I continued to read this article, I was shocked to see others who had spent so much money on different things. As I flipped through the pages, I noticed another guy who is a lot like King Ahasuerus.

His name is Prince Hans Adam II. He lives in a small country known as Liechtenstein. He spent $36 million on a piece of furniture. This piece is from the 18th century, known as the Badminton Cabinet. It is made of Florentine ebony. It is adorned with precious stones such as lapis lazuli, agate, and amethyst quartz.

When I walked across the mosaic floor this cabinet came to mind. Sitting at the long table, I started looking around and noticed this royal party is not much different from the parties held in today's culture. Alcohol and wine are free-flowing. I have my Bible with me, so I open it up to look in Esther 1. In verse 7 it says, "the royal wine was abundant." Wealth, wine, worldly treasures, and pleasures are excessive during this party. Six months of partying have moved at a reasonably brisk pace. By the end of the 180 days, the king is doing his best to influence all of his guests with his power and wealth. On the very last day, he rose to his feet and said,

"Since this party has been a great success, I have decided to lengthen this party for another seven days. I am inviting all the men of Susa to come and celebrate with us. We are celebrating those who have worked so hard to make this party a booming success. Enjoy yourself and the party. By the way, drink as much as you want."

PARTY TIME WITH THE QUEEN-BANQUET #3

The king has already granted me permission to make myself at home, so, I take it upon myself to roam the halls of the palace. The party was in full swing. As I started walking around, I began taking notes. I walk around a corner I hear women talking. I follow the sound, finding myself in another banquet room. Within, I see Queen Vashti and many women. I step back out into the corridor to scribble a few notes when I hear footsteps. Coming directly towards me are seven eunuchs. Initially, I think they are coming for me, but when they came right upon me, they entered the banquet room. One of the eunuchs named Bigtha says, "Your Majesty, the king has demanded your presence at once." Then he whispers to her the rest of the conversation. She says, "Excuse me, I am giving a party and cannot come." They don't argue with her. They head back to the banquet of the king. Feeling there is tension and trouble brewing, I follow these men back to the party. As I enter, I watch as these eunuchs walk over to the king. He is talking loud, his speech is somewhat slurred. I can tell, he has had too much to drink. The eunuchs lean over and say something to him. Angered, he shouts, "What do you mean she isn't coming? This is a command, not a request."

The room becomes silent in an instant. He paces the floor mumbling to his eunuchs. I hear him say, "All I want is for her to come in here, to show everyone, how beautiful she is."

The king is clearly drunk. He desires his wife to come in and parade herself around in front of all these men. In his rage, he shouts, "My wife is breathtakingly beautiful, yet, she has refused to come in."

He is furious. I guess he didn't think he had impressed everyone enough, so he thought if he brought the queen in, and if they saw how beautiful she is, they would really be impressed.

PROTEST AND REFUSAL

She isn't impressed. She knows he is drunk. She also knows her husband. She knows that if he was sober, he would have never demanded such an action. Clearly, she is insulted, so she refuses. All he has done up to this point is try to impress everyone with this 187-day banquet. As he sits down, still fuming, all he can think about now is how she has refused. He believes the sole thing these people will remember is that the queen refused his command. I sit in silence along with many others. All of us watch him; we notice how angry he is. Flipping back to Esther 1, I read these words, "his anger burned within him."

I take out my notebook to record all of the events that have just taken place. I write these words, "So after this long, joyous party, the king loses his cool, acts ridiculous, and very childish."

PROCLOMATION OF THE KING

The party is over. 187 days of feasting and drinking has ended. I watch as many start leaving. I sit at the table for a moment. I watch as his anger overrides his emotions. His over-inflated ego is wounded. He motions for his seven wise counselors. I move in closer to overhear the discussion. I hear Memucan say, "King Ahasuerus, you need to IMPEACH the queen. You need to find a new queen. She has insulted you, but not only you, but she has also insulted us as well. If other women hear of this news, they will start treating their husbands the same way. Things are going to get out of control, and we are going to have a bunch of angry women in the city. Not one of them will listen to their husband."

I listen intently, writing down the words I just heard. I start thinking to myself, *"Wow, these guys are your wise counselors? I believe they are blowing this way out of proportion."*

These counselors weren't interested in issuing excellent advice to the king; they were merely interested in keeping their jobs by charming him.

I observe the king. I can tell by his expression he is delighted in what he is hearing. So he immediately does exactly what Memucan has proposed. The king gathers a few scribes to record these words, "I hereby order, Queen Vashti to be impeached. I also order that ALL men be the master of their own house. ALL men will make sure their wives know whatever he says, goes!"

The proclamation was set. The scribes recorded it in every language so that it could be handed out in every province.

The events that had taken place left me stunned. I was "blown away" by the order that had been decreed.

I start heading out of the palace when Memucan stops me. "Hey, where are you going?"

"Oh, I am going to find a place to stay."

"You can stay here," Memucan says. "We have plenty of room in the palace." He leads me to a beautiful room, with a large bed, a desk, my own private restroom, and complimentary food and drink, with a servant at my disposal.

As I place my things down, I sit at the desk and start writing. I open up my notebook and write. The first sentence I write says, "Wow, this king is not as powerful as he thinks he is. Why? Because he is easily influenced by these so-called wise men." When I heard the conversation with the king, I noticed that these counselors were so ludicrous in their treatment of the queen, that they actually believe all men should be like the king, and control their homes on the basis of an executive order. The second thing I write down is how King Ahasuerus is motivated by power, anger, and revenge. He gets rid of his wife because she refused to be insulted. He became drunk, then sought advice from seven men who were also drunk. I talk to my servant for a moment, informing him that I am going to walk around the city for a while and take in some sights.

Walking through the streets, I notice bulletins all over the city. I stop in a small store on a corner and talk to the clerk inside. I ask him if he has heard any news regarding the queen. He says, "Yes, news travels swiftly around here." I ask, "Is the queen banished completely from the palace?" He says, "Yes, she most likely will also be," then he runs his finger across the front of his throat.

I take in a few more sights as I write a few more things in my notebook. With all the events that have taken place this night, I can't help but wonder what kind of things we need to learn about for our lives. So I begin to make an outline.

POINTS TO CONSIDER

#1-HISTORY OF KING AHASUERUS

King Ahasuerus is also known as King Xerxes. Xerxes is the grandson of Cyrus the Great. Cyrus was the king who had allowed the Jewish people to return home after the Babylonians had captured them and destroyed Jerusalem. The books in the Bible that talk about the terrible time of captivity are Daniel, Jeremiah, Ezekiel, and Isaiah. After some Jews had returned home to rebuild the temple, there were others who had decided to stay. You can read about the rebuilding of the temple in the books of Ezra and Nehemiah. Many people like King Xerxes. His family had been kind to the Jews, so they believed that this trend would stick around for a while. But just because the king seemed nice, doesn't mean he was a feeble or unworthy opponent when it came to war. The movie titled, "300" is loosely based on the events surrounding King Xerxes. In the movie, Xerxes is the king who they were fighting against. The Persian army was exceptionally large with nearly half a million soldiers.

#2-HEROINE/QUEEN VASHTI

Often times when we are telling the story of Esther, we hold Queen Esther in high regard, and of course, we should. Many want to place Queen Vashti on a lower rung of the ladder than of Esther. But let's look at who she was and how her actions led to her impeachment. Her name means, "beautiful woman." Obviously, she was very beautiful and her physical appearance was also lovely, that is why her drunken husband wanted to "display" her in front of all these men. There are times when the telling of the story in Esther, many focus on Vashti and the fact she was disobedient to the king. But if we take a more thorough look, yes, she disobeyed his ridiculous order, but we have to look at her modesty and her strength. She chose to be *deposed* rather than be *disgraced*. Her *dishonor* also brought about *divorce*. Amid the tragic darkness, Queen Vashti, disappeared like a shining shadow. Some believe she was merely banished from the kingdom, but in a time, when it was so wrong to go against the king, there are some who believe she was not only *expelled* from the kingdom but she was also *executed*.

POINTS OF APPLICATION

POA #1-CERTAIN situations always require a CHOICE

Four things I believe the story of Esther teaches us. It is a story of *risk, redemption, reversals,* and *restraint.* The king has spent 187 days showing off his wealth with a party. The people in attendance saw the glories of the palace; they were invited to indulge in the festivities by drinking as much wine as they wanted. They enjoyed the party by doing what they wanted when they wanted. They didn't even consider the consequences of their actions. There were others who resolved to think about what they were doing, using good judgment and common sense. The same goes for us. We always have a choice when we are put in certain situations. I remember as a young teenager, my parents tried to stress this point to me many times over. They would consistently say, "you don't have to do what everyone else is doing." Then they would add, "If they jumped off a cliff, would you jump off with them?" In other words, just because the majority of the people are doing it doesn't mean we have to join them.

POA #2- The CULTURE of today mirrors the CULTURE of the Persians

    Believe it or not, since the days of the Persians not very much has changed when it comes to the world. Look at the world of the king, it consisted of riches, influence, pleasure, gratification, and control. Our culture desires us to grab hold of the very same things. I am sure there are many times when we have given in to those demands. Let's stop and think about this for a moment. Have you ever tried making an impression on someone with your talent or with the new car you purchased? Have you ever exaggerated your story to make yourself look better? *I worked with a guy some years ago at an oil company. He was always telling stories about his farm. He told of how much money he possessed, how many cattle he owned, and how much money the bank was loaning him to purchase more property. If you would tell a story, he would always top it with a better story of his own.* How many times have we looked across the street at the neighbor's house and thought, "Wow, if I had their new truck, I would be happy?" Maybe it's not a truck, or a house, or money. Maybe for you, it's a job, a relationship, a better body, or approval from a friend. We might not want to be as rich as King Ahasuerus, but for most of us, there is a certain thing we think we need for our lives to be better.

POA #3-To CHASE after worldly things is unwise

    At the end of this chapter, you can read Esther 1. Take the time to read it and take notice of the king's reaction when the 187-day party comes to a close. He is furious, angry, and very unhappy. All the parties, all the festivities, all the wine was not enough to satisfy him. Now let's look at us. If we are striving to be satisfied by the things of this world, well, it's not going to happen. Maybe you think you will be happy if:

✧ You chase after more money in your bank account, we all need money to pay bills and such, but chasing after those green dollar bills won't make you happy
✧ You chase after material things such as a new house, new clothes, new shoes or a new look
✧ You chase after your job. Did you know Americans work more hours and receive fewer vacations than most of the world?
✧ You chase after approval from others, you should be chasing after God's approval
✧ You chase after certain people, if you are working really hard to keep someone as your friend, then it might be time to let that person go

Many who read the book of Esther see the story only as a historical event. Others see it more as a drama that is being played out with some major characters. But the story of Esther is actually a story about irony, reversals, and exaggerations. Esther is an exciting, emotional, and perplexing story. If we merely read the story of Esther at face value, if we don't dig a little deeper into the story we will ultimately miss the things that God is trying to teach us. When the queen didn't come when called upon, the king didn't try to understand why, he just got angry, threw a fit, and banished her from the kingdom, he conceivably had her executed. Therefore as we take some time to dive into the story of Esther, let's look at the why and how behind it, so that we will see what God has for us.

"These events took place during the days of Ahasuerus, who ruled 127 provinces from India to Cush. In those days King Ahasuerus reigned from his royal throne in the fortress at Susa. He held a feast in the third year of his reign for all his officials and staff, the army of Persia and Media, the nobles, and the officials from the provinces. He displayed the glorious wealth of his kingdom and the magnificent splendor of his greatness for a total of 180 days. At the end of this time, the king held a week-long banquet in the garden courtyard of the royal palace for all the people, from the greatest to the least, who were present in the fortress of Susa. White and violet linen hangings were fastened with fine white and purple linen cords to silver rods on marble columns. Gold and silver couches were arranged on a mosaic pavement of red feldspar, marble, mother-of-pearl, and precious stones. Beverages were served in an array of gold goblets, each with a different design. Royal wine flowed freely, according to the king's bounty and no restraint was placed on the drinking. The king had ordered every wine steward in his household to serve as much as each person wanted Queen Vashti also gave a feast for the women of King Ahasuerus's palace. On the seventh day, when the king was feeling good from the wine, Ahasuerus commanded Mehuman, Biztha, Harbona, Bigtha, Abagtha, Zethar, and Carkas, the seven eunuchs who personally served him, to bring Queen Vashti before him with her royal crown. He wanted to show off her beauty to the people and the officials, because she was very beautiful. But Queen Vashti refused to come at the king's command that was delivered by his eunuchs. The king became furious and his anger burned within him. The king consulted the wise men who understood the times, for it was his *normal procedure to confer with experts in law and justice. The most trusted ones were Carshena, Shethar, Admatha, Tarshish, Meres, Marsena, and Memucan. They were the seven officials of Persia and Media who had personal access to the king and occupied the highest positions in the kingdom. The king asked, 'According to the law, what should be done with Queen Vashti, since she refused to obey King Ahasuerus's command that was delivered by the eunuchs?' Memucan said in the presence of the king and his officials, 'Queen Vashti has wronged not only the king, but all the officials and the peoples who are in every one of King Ahasuerus's provinces. For the queen's action will become public knowledge to all the women and cause them to despise their husbands and say, 'King Ahasuerus ordered Queen Vashti brought before him, but she did not come.' Before this day is over, the noble women of Persia and Media who hear about the queen's act will say the same thing to all the king's officials, resulting in more contempt and fury. "If it meets the king's approval, he should personally issue a royal decree. Let it be recorded in the laws of Persia and Media, so that it cannot be revoked: Vashti is not to enter King Ahasuerus's presence, and her royal position is to be given to another woman who is more worthy than she. The decree the king issues will be heard throughout his vast kingdom, so all women will honor their husbands, from the least to the greatest."The king and his counselors approved the proposal, and he followed Memucan's advice. He sent letters to all the royal provinces, to each province in its own script and to each ethnic group in its own language, that every man should be master of his own house and speak in the language of his own people"* (Esther 1 HCSB).

Chapter 2 - "Elected"
Esther 2

PROSPECTS FOR THE KING

So far, I am intrigued by this king, the counselors, and the events that have taken place. The king wants a story, so I know I am here for the long haul. I don't know it at the time, but I am in for quite a few more surprising events.

I leave the palace early in the morning, heading for the nearest cafe. As I am seated, I look out the window and notice a massive army gathering in the streets. Apparently, the king did an outstanding job impressing the military leaders. I see men dressed in their armor, some on horses, some in chariots. I assume they are headed to war against Greece.

Things go relatively ordinary for the next two years considering there is no queen and the king is at war.

Before long, news of the king's return reverberates through the halls of the palace. It is the main conversation in the streets. The local newspaper headline reads, "PERSIA HAS BEEN DEFEATED BY GREECE."

Sitting in my room, I hear some noise in the hallway. I poke my head out the door to see who is coming. I see Memucan coming, he says, "The king is in the library, he is feeling depressed."
"Should I go to the library?" I ask.
"Sure, he knows you are writing a story. It shouldn't be a problem."

I walk into the library. The king is sitting at an ornate table. His rage has subsided. He is staring at the palace walls, looking at the vast array of scrolls. I am unsure if I should approach the king so I wait. He instantly notices me and motions for me to come and sit with him. I say, "Your Majesty, the King, I do not want to interrupt your thoughts, but you don't look like you are feeling too well."

He answers, "I can't believe we lost the war."

"I'm sorry!"

He asks me, "How is the story so far?"

"It is going well, taking many notes," I say.

In a low tone, the king says, "You know that was a great party a few years ago. I can't believe how it ended. We haven't had a queen for a long time."

I merely nod my head in agreement. He continues telling me about Queen Vashti and how she refused his command. He leans back in his chair, staring at the ceiling. I observe him as his face shows regret. He leans forwards, motions to one of his servants, and says, "Bring my attendants."

The servant leaves. Before long, he comes back with some attendants. He looks at them and says, "We do not have a queen, I was angry, I banished her. What should we do?"

Initially, they look at him with blank stares, when one of them says, "We have a plan!"

"Well, don't keep it within yourself, please share," the king says in haste.

One thing I already know about the king is that he is always ready to seek the advice of others. It is relatively standard for a king to hire wise counselors to aid him in making decisions, but as I watch these men, this seems somewhat different. These men, once again, don't seem like they are planning on handing out some excellent advice, they are insecure about their jobs, so they just tell him what they think he wants to hear. Plus, they don't want to end up like Queen Vashti.

King Ahasuerus keeps these men around because he knows they are swift to tell him what he desires to hear, not what he needs to hear. Therefore, I listen as they lay out their plan.

"Your Majesty, the king! Let's go through the neighborhoods; we will gather all the young virgins and bring them to you. We will clean them up, give them some make-up to wear, array them in some fine clothes. After a period of time, each one will come into your bedroom, one at a time. When you find the one that is most appealing to you, she can be your queen."
The king says, "What a great plan!" So he agrees. The plan is put into effect immediately.

I make my way back to my room. I decide once again to take a walk through the city, it helps me think. Walking the streets, I watch as men are stopping at each house to seize the young virgins taking them to the palace. I soon find myself in a small neighborhood. As I turn the corner, I hear a conversation between a young woman and an older gentleman. As I am listening to them speak, I can tell they are Jewish. The young girl says, "Mordecai, I know you have heard the news, but I'm afraid."
"I know you are Hadassah, but it is the king's orders." He says, "Look, we have been seized before. You know, I won't allow anything bad to happen to you. I have cared for you since your parents died. I have always treated you as my own daughter."
She responds, "Cousin, I know you have always taken care of me. But I am unhappy about this."
Mordecai says, "Hadassah, we will make the best of this situation. To start with, we will need to change your name. Let's see. I believe Esther is an excellent Persian name. From now on, you will be Esther!"

She sits down at the table. As I peak through the window, I observe as the old man places his hand on top of hers and says, "One other thing, if you are taken to the palace, make sure you do not tell them you are a Jew. Do not even tell them of your background or where you are from." With tears in her eyes, she nods her head in agreement.

PROCEDURES AND PREPARATIONS-PLOT #1

As I turn to leave, to head back to the palace. I see some men coming my way. I watch as they knock on the old man's door. He opens, they forcefully take Esther with them. I follow them. My curiosity is piqued as I observe Esther. Will she be silent? Will she enter the palace willingly? At this point, I'm thinking she really doesn't have much of a choice.

When I arrive at the palace, I notice many young women. I make my way to my room for a while so I can write a few things down. Many in the palace recognize who I am by now, so no questions are ever asked. My servant informs me that I am wanted by Memucan.

When I arrive at Memucan's room, he takes me to a larger room where all the young virgins have gathered. I watch as a man, named Hegai, enters the room. There are some other men there as well. Each one of these men is in charge of a particular harem. Hegai starts placing each young woman into one of the harems. When he comes to Esther, he stands there for a moment looking at her. He instantly recognizes her beauty. But he also notices she is different. He doesn't perceive why, but he can tell.

As I am writing in my notebook, my attention is drawn away from it to watching Esther. She is quiet and reserved. She doesn't tell them much when asked. Each young woman is escorted to the courtyard. Many are fearful, many are uneasy, wondering what comes next. Esther is afraid, worried, but determined. As I watch her,

I notice Mordecai has arrived. He is standing at a distance, but he is watching Esther in the courtyard to see how she is doing.

I find it interesting Esther does exactly as Mordecai wants. She doesn't exactly reject her faith. She merely places a veil over it.

Hegai comes to the courtyard. He starts explaining what is going to happen next. He says, "Each one of you will spend one year in our beauty school. You will spend the first six months bathing in the oil of myrrh. You will spend the last six months being adorned with make-up and perfume. We will also alter what you will eat. At the end of the year, each one of you will have a night with the king. When it is your turn to go into the king, you can take anything from the harem that you want. You will go into him in the evening. You will return the next morning. You will then be placed in another harem. If the king is delighted with you, he will call you back. If not, you will stay with your harem. These are the rules; you must follow these rules."

I watch intently as some of these young women seemed excited after hearing the rules, some of them seemed overwhelmed, others were crying, many were terrified.

I walk over to Hegai. I ask him, "Excuse me, but is there a possibility, I could talk to some of these women?" He nods his head in agreement. Naturally, the first woman I desire to talk to is Esther.

I walk over to Esther. She is exquisitely radiant. I am thinking she doesn't need this beauty school. I ask her, "Excuse me, but I am writing a story about the king, I am wondering if you would have a few minutes where we can talk?"

"Sure," she responds. "But you should probably ask Hegai first."

"I have already spoken with him," I inform her.

We sit on one of the marble benches. While looking at the beautiful courtyard, I ask, "How did you feel when they came and took you from your home?" "I was terrified at first, but after I got here, it doesn't seem that severe."

"Why is that?" I inquire.

"Ever since I was a little girl, I have had to make the best of challenging situations, so this one is no different."

As we were talking, we were interrupted by Hegai. "It is time for these young women to go their first beauty treatment," he says.

Esther doesn't seem like one who shy's away from a challenge. Every day, along with Mordecai, I come here to this garden to see how she is doing. Hegai is so pleased with the progress of Esther he is extremely impressed. Matter of fact, the rest of those who are in charge of the different harems are equally impressed by Esther. After observing her for this entire year, I believe she has bought into the idea of being in the palace. She has won the favor of everyone. She has seized this opportunity. She is holding on tight to the principles of the Persian kingdom. She has excelled more than any other woman.

PICKED BY THE KING-BANQUET #4

Since being here, I have made friends with many unique people including the king. The guards at the front gate recognize who I am. Memucan talks to me almost every day, offering me some more insight into the king. I have even made friends with Mordecai. I have even spoken to Esther on occasion. She still won't tell me about her childhood.

I awake early today. The first person I see is Hegai, he informs me that tonight is the night for Esther. I watch her throughout the day for her final preparation. She is prepared.

She can take anything from the harem with her into the king, but she only takes what Hegai suggests. As night time draws near, she is escorted to the king's chambers.

After talking to many people throughout the day, I walk through the city in the evening. I head back to my room to get some much-needed rest.

Early the next morning, I am greeted by a few servants. One of them says, "Have you heard the news?"

"No, not yet, what is the news?"

With excitement, they both say in unison, "Esther is the new queen."

About that time, I see Hegai coming around the corner. He has a big smile on his face. I stop him. He grasps my arms and says, "Esther has won the heart of the king. He favors her more."

"That is thrilling, I need to talk to someone, so I can write these things down."

Hegai says, "You will have your chance, there is a party this afternoon."

After a few brief hours, the party has started. Feasting, drinking, dancing, everyone is thrilled. King Ahasuerus comes in with his new queen. He is radiant. She is beautiful. He stands in the center of the banquet hall and says, "Esther, has won my heart. I love her. I love her beauty, her grace, her kindness, and her simplicity." He then turns to Esther, placing the royal crown upon her head, signifying to all that she is the new queen.

The king pulls out all the stops for this party. He invites the staff, the counselors, the officials. This party is for Esther. In the back of my mind, I am thinking,

"Let's hope this party doesn't end as the previous one did."

This party is so special the king lets the provinces skip their taxes. He is so excited that he hands out gifts. The party lasts way into the night. When the party is winding down, I head back to my room to write a few things down.

PRESERVING OF THE KING

Awakened by a noise in the hallway, I find myself standing in the hallway. I decide today would be a good day to talk to Esther, now that she is queen. I am certain the king won't mind. As I make my way down the hallway towards the king's quarters, I discover a room that I haven't noticed before. I step inside and see Mordecai. He is happy, of course; he is always happy, but today I'm sure he is happier than normal. I ask him, "Mordecai, what are you doing here?"

He says, "I work here, didn't you know?"

"No, I believe you have failed to convey that information."

"Yes, this is my office, it is dubbed the king's gate. I come here every day to do my job."

"What job is that?" I asked inquisitively.

"I am one of the officials in the king's administration."

I look around in Mordecai's workspace. I notice a desk, some scrolls, and a few chairs. He says, "If you will excuse me, I need to get back to work."

"No problem," I say.

While he is sitting at his desk, not too far away there are two officers standing in the hallway having a discussion. Mordecai observes these two men. They seem angry, making frantic motions with their hands. Mordecai goes to the doorway, he overhears them plotting to kill the king. Immediately, Mordecai calls for one of Esther's servants. He is ushered to Esther where he informs her about the plot to assassinate the king. Esther goes to the king right away, she notifies him of the plan. She says, "We would not have known about this plan if it wasn't for Mordecai." As soon as these words escaped her lips, the king commences an investigation. He finds out that the words are accurate, he has both of these men put to death. He calls for the scribes, who record all these things in the chronicles. As soon as I learn of the execution, I head back to my room to record my own thoughts.

POINTS TO CONSIDER

There are many alternative views in regards to the words "and the king LOVED Esther," in verse 17 of chapter 2. Before we look at that phrase let's go back a few verses to see if some wording will help us analyze the phrase above. It was explained to each woman that they would have one night with the king. The scripture says the young virgin would go into the king's quarters in the evening and not return until morning. This indicates to us an automatic belief that she went in, not to play a board game of some kind, or just to talk, but for sex. As far back as I can remember, I have never heard one teacher, or one preacher talk about this aspect of Esther. Many times we would only just hear that the king loved Esther. She found grace and favor more than all the women, therefore, he chose her as queen. But let's dig a little deeper.

*VIEW #1-*Let's take a look at the Hebrew word and definition for the word, "LOVED." The Hebrew word is: 'ahab. The definition offered in the Strongs Concordance is, "to have affection for (sexually or otherwise).[1] This definition would lead one to believe that when Esther entered into the king's chambers, a sexual encounter would have occurred.

VIEW #2-If she went into the king's bedroom, spent the night with him, including sex, then one might challenge the integrity of Esther. One might also want to believe that Esther has compromised her faith. Therefore, the question begs to be asked, "Did she have a choice?" The answer, I believe that fits here is, "Yes and No!" Let's think about the events, that took place before she stepped inside the king's chamber. She was carried away from her home. Mordecai advises her to conceal her identity, giving her a new name. She is placed in a harem, told to follow certain rules and procedures. She was equally told that she would have to go into the king's chamber.

This brings us to her choice. In reality, she did not have a choice when she was taken from her home. She could have told Hegai who she was, going against Mordecai, but since she didn't she made a choice to keep her faith hidden. This would lead us to believe she compromised. Clearly Mordecai was concerned for her safety. This is why he went to the garden every day to check on her. She went through the beauty treatments, ate their food, wore their clothes. This would be the next compromise in the list of events. When her time arrived to go to the king, she did exactly as she was told to do. This is, furthermore, a compromise. But as we have already seen, this king, is not the most prime example when it comes to morality. Now at this point, you might be getting the idea that I am criticizing Esther for her actions. You might actually feel insulted that I would see Esther in the above light. Esther grappled with a true dilemma. I don't know her thoughts, but she might have wished she could have stayed with the name Hadassah. She might have hoped that she could have stayed in her home with Mordecai. The fact is, she had a choice. She could have put God first and suffered whatever consequences that would have come with her choice, or she could conceal her identity, follow the rules of this pagan king, make the best of a complex decision, believing that God would work it all out.

Just for a moment, let's consider the other option of her choice. We have already noted that as far as her choice, when she was taken from her home, there wasn't much of a choice in that situation. When she arrived at the palace, she could have told everyone who she really was, declined the beauty treatments, food, and clothes. She could have denied spending the night with the king. I would assume this would have come at a substantial cost. She more than likely would not have been chosen queen, therefore, we would not be compiling a story about Queen Esther.

*VIEW #3-*Let's take a look at the king in all of this. As we have already seen he is obsessed with outward beauty. Just look at the palace. Marble columns, fancy floors, couches of gold, and fine linens. In the first banquet, we noted he was obsessed with his wife's beauty as well, wanting to parade her in front of thousands of men. After he returns from the war with Greece, we watch as he harbors regret but instantly dismisses it upon the advice of his counselors. Look a little closer at their advice. The woman who was going to replace Vashti had to be beautiful, young, and a virgin. He is wealthy, powerful, and has an enormous ego. Since King Ahasuerus was obsessed with outward beauty he found it easy to "dump" one queen to gain another. His goal is to get the most gorgeous wife possible, so he loves the idea of having women come into his chambers, so he can try them out one at a time. It was part of the procedure to go into his chambers, even if they didn't want to spend the night with him. So he raped them. With the king's order, these women were abducted from their homes, sent through a rigorous beauty treatment plan, placed inside a harem. After her one night, if she is not called upon again, she is taken to another harem. She would now be enslaved inside the palace walls. She would never be able to go back to her family. Hence, we see a king, who abducted women, sent them through a beauty school if they didn't meet his requirements of beauty, they were tossed aside to be incarcerated within his kingdom.

All of the points above are plausible when you look at the events that occurred. Regardless of which view you believe, the scripture is clear that Mordecai had her withhold her background so that she would remain undetected as a Jew until her appointed time. With the odds stacked against her, she obtains favor with the king. She is walking the runway, a sash around her shoulder, an imperial crown on her head. Even though Esther has won, she knows what kind of man he is. She knows that if she slips up, he will be finished with her, just as he was with Vashti. She can look around the palace and notice there are many other attractive women who would be next in line to take her place.

POINTS OF APPLICATION

POA #1-Who is in our CIRCLE?

As I reflect back, one thing I realize about King Ahasuerus, which we have noted before, is that he is always willing to receive advice from his advisers. The king is a powerful king, but his circle of advisers and counselors are most likely not the best to be dispensing advice. These men, who are in his circle, are unwilling to tell him what he needs to hear, the hard things, the difficult things, they just tell him the things he wants to hear. What about you and I, who is in our circle? Do we have people in our lives who are able to tell us the difficult and uncomfortable things? There are many times when we want them to tell us the easy things. It is hard to receive information from someone that challenges us, or forces us past our limits, or calls us out concerning our flaws. The king in the palace, lived below his potential as a ruler over Persia. Why? Because he is self-indulgent, arrogant, and he surrounds himself with weak individuals that cater to what he desires to hear. If we surround ourselves with people who tell us what we want to hear, then we will live just like the king, we will live way below our potential, missing out on what God has for us.

POA #2-How do we keep our CONVICTIONS in a CULTURE that doesn't share our beliefs?

The Jews living in Persia wrestled with this dilemma every day. We face this most every day in our lives. Many of us discover this to be a true dilemma. Therefore how do we stay faithful to God in a culture that doesn't believe in God? First, we must be totally committed and dependent upon God. We must also realize that He WILL fulfill His promises. Second, we must know we are like the Jews, we are living as exiles in a foreign land. Therefore, we must not get too attached to this world. We have to avoid blending into the environment in which we live. Third, we must know that God is directing all of life's circumstances. He will consistently place us where we are better fit to serve Him. Fourth, we must know that God is constantly working behind the scenes even when we can't see Him.

POA #3-Are we being CARRIED away?

In Esther 2, we see the two words "carried away" mentioned three times in the same verse. Mordecai, the Jew, had been carried away from Jerusalem with other captives, who were also carried away, with a king who had been carried away by the Babylonians. When we look at Esther's life so far, we can also include these two words. Esther had been carried away from Jerusalem. She is now living in Persia, previously known as Babylon. She is now being carried away from her small home in Persia to the palace. Then, she is carried away from the harem to the king's bed to see if she is pleasing enough for him to call her queen. How many times have we been "carried away" by our lust? James 1:14 says, **"But each person is tempted when he is carried away and enticed by his own evil desires"(HCSB).** When we take a more thorough look at this king, he has enslaved women. He sleeps with a different one every night, and we consider him a cruel beast. Yet, how many of us live in secret by allowing an anonymous person into our homes via our computer or phone, using that person for our personal satisfaction?

POA #4-Are we COMPROMISING?

Compromise? What does it look like? Do we not talk about God because we are fearful of losing a friend? Do we embrace the world's values instead of godly values? Do we construct our own plan, believing it is the best plan, whether we see God working or not? As we have already talked about, some believe Esther compromised by concealing her faith, by allowing them to try and make her more beautiful, and by sleeping with the king. Whatever you decide to believe about Esther, God nevertheless used her. The Bible is full of stories about tremendous men and women of God who compromised, yet God, nonetheless, utilized them. Why? Because God can take our compromises, our failures, our sins, and transform us to be used for His glory. Abraham lied. Moses murdered. Samson's lust was out of control. David committed adultery, then had someone murdered. Peter denied Jesus. Esther possibly was not as good as we initially thought. But in reality, none of us are.

POA #5-Are we CAPTIVATED by beauty?

The king, the Persians, were obviously obsessed with the outward appearance. The king demanded to have the most beautiful woman by his side. Obsession is seen in the fact, that each young virgin spent one year in a beautifying treatment regimen. Matter of fact, if the king didn't think the woman was beautiful enough, he had her go back to the harem and try for the next one. How often have we seen this in our culture? Our world is not much diverse from the Persians. We are obsessed with the unrealistic requirements of beauty. Do we find ourselves in this trap? Do we evaluate people based on their appearance? Do we judge ourselves by our appearance? How about you? When you look in the mirror, do you feel great when you look good but sad then you don't? Do you constantly seek approval from others based on how they perceive you physically?

Ian Duguid composed these words, *"Women almost always fall short of standards that are expected of them regarding physical appearance. Particularly for women, it is difficult to go through a day without viewing images that send the message, "you're not good enough." The pervasiveness of the media makes it very challenging for most women to avoid evaluating themselves against the sociocultural standard of beauty."* [2]

In one article the authors wrote these words, *"The Psychological effects of the pursuit of the perfect female body include unhappiness, confusion, misery and insecurity. Women often believe that if only they had perfect looks, their lives would be perfectly happy; they blame their unhappiness on their bodies."* [3]

A problem arises when we rate people by their outward appearance, they become replaceable. This is one of the reasons why divorce and affairs are excessive in our society. The king considered it no problem replacing Vashti. Look at the king's process to select a new queen. If he is uncertain, he disregards one, and tries another one. Always believing someone else much better will come along.

POA #6-What can CHANGE your worth?

The straightforward answer is NOTHING! Esther knew who she was, she knew her value. With all the perfumes, beauty treatments, and gifts, she didn't change. Esther was the daughter of the true King, and for her, that was enough. Guess what? Nothing can change our value. People may come along and try to crush us; they will disappoint us, they will stomp on our hopes and dreams, but we are still valuable. Remember, no matter what happens in life, nothing can take away the value God has given to us.

Esther, selected as the new queen because God had a plan, despite her compromise. God has a plan for each one of us, despite our failures and compromises of the past. God transformed her and used her. God can transform us and use us.

"Some time later, when King Ahasuerus's rage had cooled down, he remembered Vashti, what she had done, and what was decided against her. The king's personal attendants suggested, 'Let a search be made for beautiful young women for the king. Let the king appoint commissioners in each province of his kingdom, so that they may assemble all the beautiful young women to the harem at the fortress of Susa. Put them under the care of Hegai, the king's eunuch, who is in charge of the women, and give them the required beauty treatments. Then the young woman who pleases the king will become queen instead of Vashti.' This suggestion pleased the king, and he did accordingly. In the fortress of Susa, there was a Jewish man named Mordecai son of Jair, son of Shimei, son of Kish, a Benjaminite. He had been taken into exile from Jerusalem with the other captives when King Nebuchadnezzar of Babylon took King Jeconiah of Judah into exile. Mordecai was the legal guardian of his cousin Hadassah (that is, Esther), because she didn't have a father or mother. The young woman had a beautiful figure and was extremely good-looking. When her father and mother died, Mordecai had adopted her as his own daughter.

When the king's command and edict became public knowledge, many young women gathered at the fortress of Susa under Hegai's care. Esther was also taken to the palace and placed under the care of Hegai, who was in charge of the women. The young woman pleased him and gained his favor so that he accelerated the process of the beauty treatments and the special diet that she received. He assigned seven hand-picked female servants to her from the palace and transferred her and her servants to the harem's best quarters. Esther did not reveal her ethnic background or her birthplace, because Mordecai had ordered her not to. Every day Mordecai took a walk in front of the harem's courtyard to learn how Esther was doing and to see what was happening to her. During the year before each young woman's turn to go to King Ahasuerus, the harem regulation required her to receive beauty treatments with oil of myrrh for six months and then with perfumes and cosmetics for another six months. When the young woman would go to the king, she was given whatever she requested to take with her from the harem to the palace. She would go in the evening, and in the morning she would return to a second harem under the supervision of Shaashgaz, the king's eunuch in charge of the concubines. She never went to the king again, unless he desired her and summoned her by name. Esther was the daughter of Abihail, the uncle of Mordecai who had adopted her as his own daughter. When her turn came to go to the king, she did not ask for anything except what Hegai, the king's trusted official in charge of the harem, suggested. Esther won approval in the sight of everyone who saw her. She was taken to King Ahasuerus in the royal palace in the tenth month, the month Tebeth, in the seventh year of his reign. The king loved Esther more than all the other women. She won more favor and approval from him than did any of the other young women. He placed the royal crown on her head and made her queen in place of Vashti. The king held a great banquet for all his officials and staff. It was Esther's banquet. He freed his provinces from tax payments and gave gifts worthy of the king's bounty. When the young women were assembled together for a second time, Mordecai was sitting at the King's Gate.Esther still had not revealed her birthplace or her ethnic background, as Mordecai had directed. She obeyed Mordecai's orders, as she always had while he raised her. During those days while Mordecai *was sitting at the King's Gate, Bigthan and Teresh, two eunuchs who guarded the king's entrance, became infuriated and planned to assassinate King Ahasuerus. When Mordecai learned of the plot, he reported it to Queen Esther, and she told the king on Mordecai's behalf. When the report was investigated and verified, both men were hanged on the gallows. This event was recorded in the Historical Record in the king's presence"(Esther 2 HCSB).*

Chapter 3 - "Hated"
Esther 3

POSSESSING HATE FOR MORDECAI-PLOT #2

For the next few years, everything in the palace runs quite smoothly. I spend most of my time talking to numerous individuals or staying in my room, writing. Everyone is summoned to the main banquet hall. I expect there will be another banquet. But when I arrive, a promotion is being handed out to a guy by the name of Haman. I wonder who this guy is. I haven't observed him before. I am stunned when I hear the king say, "Haman, the Agagite is second in command. This day I institute a law that all people must bow down to him." I am literally blown away. This guy just pops up out of nowhere, now the king says everyone must bow. What?

As soon as the ceremony is over, I run to my room, summon my servant to bring Memucan to me. I must find out about this guy, I am sure Memucan must know something. A short time later Memucan comes into my room. I say, "Memucan, who is this Haman guy?"
"Do you have a few minutes?" he asks.
"Sure, I didn't plan on writing about him."

As Memucan shares a little information about Haman, I search out a few others to see if I can piece it all together. Here is what I find out.

A few hundred years ago, God informed the Israelites that He would wipe out the Amalekites. King Saul, an ancestor of Mordecai was supposed to destroy the Amalekites, but he disobeyed God sparing the king, Agag. Later, the prophet Samuel went to King Saul, inquiring why he didn't do as God had commanded. Because of Saul's disobedience, Samuel took a sword and cut King Agag into pieces. Some years later, ironically some Amalekites killed King Saul. Consequently through the stories of many who I talked to, they believe that when Saul disobeyed God, sparing King Agag, he also spared some other Amalekites as well. I open my Bible to read more on this subject and learn that it has been recorded in the book of first and second Samuel. In the palace, there are descendants of King Saul, Esther, and Mordecai. Also, King Ahasuerus is honoring a descendant of Agag, Haman.

Mordecai must be feeling the sting of being passed up for a promotion or any sort of recognition. I observe him as he makes his way back to the king's gate.

Every day, Haman walks around the palace, he walks past the king's gate, everyone bows except Mordecai. The odd thing is that Haman barely notices. But a few of the servants take note that Mordecai doesn't bow down. They walk over to him and say, "Hey, what in the world are you doing? Why aren't you obeying the command of the king?"

They keep asking for a few days. Finally, one morning Mordecai gives an explanation as to why. He says, "Look, guys, I am not going to bow down because I am a Jew."

The servants beg Mordecai, they plead with him to bow down, but he continues to refuse. One afternoon, they leave, they go find Haman. When they corner him in a hallway, they bow, then they say, "Excuse us, but you know Mordecai, the guy at the king's gate, well, he refuses to bow down to you." Haman decides to see this for himself. He heads over to Mordecai's office, the king's gate. As he walks by Mordecai he watches as Mordecai doesn't bow down. Instantly, Haman is furious. His face turns red, his anger is ignited within himself.

I watch because I am baffled at what will happen. Is Haman going to lash out at Mordecai and slay him? I note the tension in the air, as they stand and stare at each other. Finally, Haman turns and walks away.

PUR/THE LOT

Since I am writing a story about the king. I stay relatively busy following many of these people around, so I can write down everything that is happening. As I am witnessing the anger and rage of Haman. I record this in my notebook: *"Haughty Haman Has a Huge Hatred for a Humble Hebrew."*

Haman is sitting in the main library trying to come up with a plan for Mordecai. He knows Mordecai is a Jew. Suddenly, it is apparent what he needs to accomplish. He says to himself, *"I won't kill Mordecai alone, I will find a way to execute all of the Jews that are living in this kingdom."*

I haven't talked to Haman yet, so here is my chance to discover what is on his mind. I walk into the library. I see Mordecai sitting there writing a few things down. I ask, "Excuse me, Haman, but would you have a few minutes?"

"What for?" he replies angrily.

"You know, I am composing a book about the king, so I want to hear what you have to say about the kingdom."

"Right now," he says, "I have a considerably more significant problem."

"Alright, I will leave you alone."

"Well, wait, maybe you can note some things down regarding this Jew, Mordecai."

I take out my notebook, ready to write when He says, "You know, Mordecai has refused to bow down to me. As a result, I won't do anything to Mordecai, I'm going to make sure every Jewish person dies."

As we sit and talked for a few more minutes, I could tell Haman is arrogant. By his words and tone, I could see his hatred for Mordecai is growing at a rapid pace. Haman, jumps out of his chair, runs out of the library, says to a few servants, "Go grab a calendar and some dice."

I stay seated in the library to see what Haman's plan is. The servants hurry back with a calendar in hand and the dice. They secure a place on one of the tables. They open up the calendar, tossing the dice. They witness them spin around, landing on a specific number. Every time they perform this; they mark off a date on the calendar. Then on the final spin of the dice, the number points to the twelfth month, and the thirteenth day. He circles the date with a big red marker. He turns to the servants and me and says, "The date is set, there will be no more Jews." I take note that the date is eleven months away.

He picks up the calendar, rolls it up, slides it under his arm. He motions for me to come with him. We head directly for the king's quarters. When we arrive, the king invites us in. Haman says, "Your majesty, the king, I have something I desire to discuss with you."
"Definitely, Haman, what would that be?"
"Well, there is an enormous group of people scattered throughout your kingdom. Their ways, their laws are different from all other people. They do not carry out your laws; it is no profit for the king to tolerate these people. If it is pleasing to you, my king, let there be a law made that all of them be destroyed. I will pay 10,000 talents of silver and have it deposited into your account."

I am standing there dumbfounded. The king doesn't submit any questions. He doesn't even try to find out who these people are. He doesn't talk about doing any sort of investigation to see how these people are breaking laws.

I watch as the king takes off his signet ring, hands it to Haman. King Ahasuerus says, "Hey, it's your money, accomplish what you desire with these people."

As I witness these events unfold, I am shocked. But I have witnessed the pride and arrogance of the king before. I am also witnessing the pride and hate that Haman has in his heart.

PROCLAMATION OF A CATASTROPHIC
EVENT-BANQUET #5-CLIFFHANGER #1

Haman leaves the king's presence with the signet ring in hand. He is walking with his chest out, head held high, smiling, knowing he has completely sold his plan to the king. Literally! He promptly drafts the new law. The law is formulated for the governors and officials in each province. The law states, "The law written herein calls for all Jews to be destroyed, killed and annihilated, young and old, women and children, in a single day. This will occur on the thirteenth day of the twelfth month, the month of Adar, and all of their goods shall be plundered." I watch as the scribes are writing the new law. Haman uses the signet ring, to seal the law.

Copies of the new law were immediately written down. These copies were produced in the language of each people in every province. A number of men and couriers arrive. They immediately take the copies and post them throughout the empire. There were many copies also posted throughout the palace.

I see Haman and the king sitting out in the courtyard. They are smiling, laughing, sipping on their wine. They lift their cups, tap them against each other, and drink some more. Haman's arrogance shines, while the king's face looks clueless. Of course, they are

46

satisfied. I head back to my room. I must write some things down for the book.

POINTS TO CONSIDER

POINT #1-PLOT OF DEATH

I lean against the wall in my room. I start to mull over all these events in my head. I can't help but think of the pride of Haman. I can't help but think about how clueless the king seems to be. Esther, still has not revealed her identity, but we know that Mordecai has. Haman is a crafty salesman. The king is a gullible customer.

Look at the plot with me again. Haman sells his violent plan to the king. His story is crafty and inaccurate. The recipe he presents is a mixture of verifiable facts, slight exaggeration, and deception.

In the mixing bowl of his story, he adds in one cup of the undeniable fact that the Jews were scattered throughout the Persian kingdom. Then, he sprinkles in some inaccuracy. Because they weren't the only one's living in Persia, they were other exiles as well. Next he adds a teaspoon of slight exaggeration. He said the Jews retained some religious laws that were different from their laws. But this is not the total truth because they equally maintained laws that were like the Persian laws. They followed the Persian laws but if their religious laws conflicted, they would keep their religious laws. Next, he added a quarter cup of deception. There was only one Jew, Mordecai, who did not keep the law of bowing down to Haman. But he made sure to proclaim to the king that all the Jews were not keeping the king's laws.

POINT #2-PLOT FOR PROFIT

One of the first things we notice is Haman doesn't ask the king to make the law, he asks the king to allow it. Therefore, what does he do? He flashes money in front of the king. Not only does Haman offer to pay. He informs the king that when they plunder the Jews, it will bring in more money for the king. Let's go back to some events that happened in the past. At the beginning of Esther, the king is wealthy, holding a 187-day party, trying to influence his financial partners to support his war with Greece. Nine years have passed since the feast. The king went to war with Greece. He lost. His bank account has an exceptionally low balance. Haman appeals to the king on the basis of his bank account being critically low. Evidently Haman has some money that he has acquired, he promises the king that he will be delighted to pay. We see his hate and his obsession to massacre the Jews.

POINT #3-PLOT FAR OFF

The law was written down, sealed with the signet ring of the king. Moreover, notice the day of execution for all Jews takes place eleven months from now. Haman and the king are relaxing, enjoying their drink, while their hearts turn callous. Haman is thinking the stars were in his favor. He believes the lot has picked the appropriate day for this catastrophe. But what he doesn't comprehend is that when God seems hidden, He is obviously working. God has caused the lot to fall far enough away that God has a lot of time to orchestrate His plan. Haman bribed the king, but God won't be bribed. Look at Proverbs 16:33, *"Make your motions and cast your votes, but GOD has the final say" (MSG).*

POINTS OF APPLICATION

POA #1-CLEAR Instructions

Haman's hatred for Mordecai caused him to seek revenge not only for Mordecai but for all of the Jews. It all started, though, because Mordecai stood his ground, believing he didn't need to obey the king's command and bow down to Haman. Were his actions justified? In the book of Romans, we are instructed that we should respect the government, but other parts of the scriptures teach, we should obey God rather than men. A thin line between these two points directs us to see that we as Christians need to obey God before anyone else. Mordecai clearly lived with this principle. Mordecai followed God, showing where his priorities were. One day we might find ourselves in a similar situation. It is hoped, we will find the grace and the courage to do it as well as Mordecai did.

POA #2-The COLD-SHOULDER

The decree had been declared by the king. In eleven months, the Persians will be able to exterminate the Jews and seize their property. As we step to the end of the chapter, we see Haman and the king has turned a cold-shoulder, they have become indifferent as they sit there and drink together in celebration. Two things come to surface here: indulgence and irony. We have identified these two things already in the book of Esther. Indulgence represents a trait of the king, now it is a trait of Haman. He was unsatisfied with seeking revenge on one man who didn't bow, he wants to take revenge on the whole Jewish race. The irony is scattered throughout the book of Esther. In this scene we see the king and Haman making a decision on their own to annihilate God's people. Yet, earlier in the book the king could not make a decision unless he received counsel from his counselors. These two men have been blinded, and their hearts have been hardened. Not only have they turned a cold-shoulder to the Jews, but they have also turned a cold-shoulder towards God. At this juncture, we identify a point that we must consider for ourselves. If we ignore God or turn a cold-shoulder towards God, then we will become blind and hardened in our hearts as well. Ultimately, those two things will usher us to actions that will cause harm to us or someone else.

POA #3- God is in CONTROL

At the writing of this book, Donald Trump will be up for re-election in a few months. I have watched as people get "up in arms" about the president, or they become furious when their candidate doesn't win. Think with me for just a moment. How would you feel if you saw a teletype roll across the bottom of your television screen informing you that you and your race was going to be eliminated forever? Look in the palace at the end of chapter three, you behold two men sipping from golden cups, while Jews all around are shaking, weeping, and crying out to God. One thing we should note here, God is in control even when it seems He is hiding. He has a plan. More precisely in the midst of our lives, there are times when we identify people who are seeking to destroy our faith and us. But we need to realize we serve a God who is able to defend us, keeping our attackers away. Nothing is "coincidental." When the lot has been cast, and it appears that the night has gotten pitch black, we must trust in God to fulfill His promises. Nothing will halt His plan.

POA #4-CONNIVING Enemy

Haman, the master conniver. He went to the king, promoted his story, literally. Even now, we encounter an enemy who is more conniving than Haman. Every day, he walks around seeking to peddle us a story, seeking to get the signet ring of our lives. Let's look at his logic for a moment. He arrives by your side as soon as you awake and says, "Hey, I know you are lonely, but trusting God is not going to take that away. You need to find a good man or a good woman, then you will be genuinely happy." At lunchtime, the enemy sits next to you and says, "Following Jesus will not satisfy you, but if you go after what you desire and attain it, then you will be truly satisfied." Remember, the devil, the enemy is explained in God's word like this: "He is like a roaring lion seeking for someone to devour." God's Word equally says, "He has come to kill, steal, and destroy." Another reason to depend on God, to know that God will keep His promise is that our enemy, the devil, will not win. God had a plan, He sent His Son Jesus so that we can be free from the POWER of sin, the PRESENCE of sin, and the PENALTY of sin.

"After all this took place, King Ahasuerus honored Haman, son of Hammedatha the Agagite. He promoted him in rank and gave him a higher position than all the other officials. The entire royal staff at the King's Gate bowed down and paid homage to Haman, because the king had commanded this to be done for him. But Mordecai would not bow down or pay homage. The members of the royal staff at the King's Gate asked Mordecai, "Why are you disobeying the king's command?" When they had warned him day after day and he still would not listen to them, they told Haman to see if Mordecai's actions would be

tolerated, since he had told them he was a Jew. When Haman saw that Mordecai was not bowing down or paying him homage, he was filled with rage. And when he learned of Mordecai's ethnic identity, Haman decided not to do away with Mordecai alone. He planned to destroy all of Mordecai's people, the Jews, throughout Ahasuerus's kingdom. In the first month, the month of Nisan, in King Ahasuerus's twelfth year, Pur (that is, the lot) was cast before Haman for each day in each month, and it fell on the twelfth month, the month Adar. Then Haman informed King Ahasuerus, 'There is one ethnic group, scattered throughout the peoples in every province of your kingdom, yet living in isolation. Their laws are different from everyone else's and they do not obey the king's laws. It is not in the king's best interest to tolerate them. If the king approves, let an order be drawn up authorizing their destruction, and I will pay 375 tons of silver to the accountants for deposit in the royal treasury.' The king removed his signet ring from his finger and gave it to Haman son of Hammedatha the Agagite, the enemy of the Jewish people. Then the king told Haman, 'The money and people are given to you to do with as you see fit' The royal scribes were summoned on the thirteenth day of the first month, and the order was written exactly as Haman commanded. It was intended for the royal satraps, the governors of each of the provinces, and the officials of each ethnic group and written for each province in its own script and to each ethnic group in its own language. It was written in the name of King Ahasuerus and sealed with the royal signet ring. Letters were sent by couriers to each of the royal provinces telling the officials to destroy, kill, and annihilate all the Jewish people—young and old, women and children—and plunder their possessions on a single day, the thirteenth day of Adar, the twelfth month. A copy of the text, issued as law throughout every province, was distributed to all the peoples so that they might get ready for that day. The couriers left, spurred on by royal command, and the law was issued in the fortress of Susa. The king and Haman sat down to drink, while the city of Susa was in confusion" (Esther 3 HCSB).

Chapter 4 - "Challenged"
Esther 4

PRAYER OF MORDECAI

As I walk through the streets of Susa the sounds I hear are deafening as many Jews are wailing, crying, weeping, and lamenting. Anxiety and nervousness keep everyone on edge. All of the Jews I see are dressed in sackcloth and ashes. I learn from a few that I talk to that this is their custom when they are in mourning. I walk back to the palace. I see that Mordecai is responding the same way as those outside the palace. Mordecai leaves the palace and heads to the streets.

As I am heading to my room, I see Queen Esther. There are a few of her attendants by her side. She tells them to go find out what is wrong with Mordecai. She gives one of the attendants a new set of clothes. He refuses the new clothes. As I am observing her and her attendant it seems to me that she is just as clueless about what is going on as her husband is. When Mordecai refuses the clothes, she sends Hathach to see if he can find out what is wrong with Mordecai.

POINT OUT THE PROBLEM

Esther's attendant Hathach walks out to the street to find Mordecai to identify what the problem is. I overhear him as he says, "Hey Mordecai, Esther has sent me out here to find out what is wrong. Can you explain it to me? I will let the queen know."

"Look, Haman and the king have executed a decree to slay all of the Jews. Here is the decree."He delivers the document to Hathach. Mordecai also tells him the price that has been paid by Haman for this order.

Mordecai says, "When you go back in and talk to Esther, make sure you explain it all to her. Compel her to go to the king, to plead for his favor and her people." So Hathach runs back to the queen and explains everything to her.

PANIC BRINGS FEAR

Esther is pacing the floor. She has been put on the spot. Mordecai's message is one of urgency. He pleads with her. After all, she is the queen; she lives in the palace, if anyone can speak to the king, it is Esther. I speak with Esther for a moment. I ask, "What are you going to do?"
She replies, "First I must send a message back to Mordecai, telling him how this all works."
"What do you mean?"
"Everyone that lives inside of this palace knows what the law concerns going before the king. We can barely go into his inner courtyard if he has called for us. If we haven't, it will be certain death. If the king extends his golden scepter then we live. I haven't been called for over thirty days."

She calls her assistant over, delivers him a piece of paper and says, "Go give this to Mordecai, make sure he reads every word."

PLEA OF MORDECAI

Sitting there in silence with Esther, her face displays signs of concern. She looks at me. I look at her. She says, "I feel trapped! I don't know what to do. Before I was chosen queen, Mordecai demanded me to keep silent, now he wants me to beg before the king because of our people. This for sure will expose me of whom I genuinely am."

Her attendant rushes back in. He tells Esther that Mordecai has read her message, but he also hands her a piece of paper. She opens it and reads, "Just because you are in the king's palace, do not believe you will be spared. If you keep silent, deliverance for our people will come from someplace else, but you along with our people will perish."

Then in bold letters she reads, "JUST THINK, MAYBE YOU HAVE BEEN MADE QUEEN FOR SUCH A TIME AS THIS!"

Esther is trembling. Fear and panic has gripped her heart. I read the words from Mordecai; he seems confident.

PROWESS OF PUGNACITY-CLIFFHANGER #2

A sudden change comes over Esther as I am sitting there writing down these messages. She says, "Mordecai has no other plan." She writes out another message to Mordecai. She hands it to her attendant and says, "Take this quickly to Mordecai."

When Mordecai receives the message, he opens up the piece of paper, he reads these words, "Go gather all of the Jews together, make sure you fast and pray. Don't eat or drink anything for three days. I, myself, and my attendants will also fast and pray. Then after three days, I will go to the king, even though it is against the law. If I die, I die."

Mordecai left and did exactly as Queen Esther has commanded.

POINTS TO CONSIDER

#1-WAS ESTHER SHELTERED, IGNORANT OR CALLOUS?

    The reason this question is presented is that when Mordecai had dressed in sackcloth and ashes, Esther seemed to be clueless. Matter of fact, the Jews throughout the whole empire knew about the edict that had been brought down against them. But for some odd reason, Esther didn't seem to know. The decree had been posted throughout the empire and in the palace. Conceivably now that she was Queen, she has decided to shut herself inside the palace forgetting about her people who lived outside of the palace, becoming sheltered. Maybe she has fallen so deep into compromise she has embraced the culture in which she now resides, which has led her to become callous. Maybe she has forgotten who she is and where she came from, she wants to pretend everything is okay, therefore, she has become ignorant of the situation her people are now facing.

#2-MORDECAI WANTS ESTHER TO TELL

    As we have seen already, the story of Esther deals with many ironies. At this moment we behold another picture of it. When the king sent men to gather up all the young virgins, Mordecai made sure that Hadassah's name was changed to Esther. He made sure Esther did not tell of her background or ethnicity. But at present, when the fate of the Jews is on the line. He wants Esther to place her life on the line, go before the king, plead with him because of her people, which in turn would cause her to be exposed.

#3-WORKING IN THE PALACE

Throughout the story of Esther, we notice Mordecai is always at the king's gate. Contrasting views have arisen at what this indeed conveys. I touched on it earlier, but let's look at how many times it is mentioned. Seven unique times we observe that Mordecai was "sitting" at the king's gate, or he was at the king's gate. Most of us would tend to believe he is sitting outside, in front of a gate, on a road that leads to the palace. One commentary says the king's gate was not just a place but a position. It is possible the king's gate is the place and position of Mordecai. It is his government job. It is his office or workplace. Hence if we hold to the belief that Mordecai is just going to work then we can notice that each time the king's gate is mentioned, he is just working, doing his job.

Since Mordecai went to work every day then we can appreciate why he was able to keep an eye on Esther when she was taken to the palace to live in a harem. Since Mordecai went to work, sitting in his office, he was able to overhear those who wanted to assassinate the king. Now, we can see Mordecai is able to encourage Esther to go before the king. Later, we will see there are two other things that happen because Mordecai went to work, at the king's gate.

#4-WILLING NOT TO OPT OUT

The key verse in the book of Esther is in chapter 4, verse 14. Mordecai says, "It is possible you were elected queen for such a time as this." Throughout this story, we have continually seen Mordecai trying to assist Esther to recognize her purpose. At this point, Mordecai is saying, "Here is where you are. This is the purpose that you are called for."

Expeditiously, let's review her journey here. Her family had been carried away from their home, placed as exiles in Babylon. Her parents ultimately died, so Mordecai took her in and raised her as his own. Babylon was eventually taken over by Persia. Esther was then taken away to the palace by King Ahasuerus. She was commanded to go through a year of beautification, then she was chosen as Queen. Presently she and her people face certain death by Haman.

Esther could have taken a glance back at her life and opted out of all of this. She could have believed her life was useless. She could look and believe God seemed hidden. But Mordecai knew that God was working behind the scenes.

POINTS OF APPLICATION

POA #1-Are we CALLOUS?

Have we chosen to be callous? Let's pause for a moment and think of Esther and Mordecai. He was bearing the weight of impending death, yet Esther barely seemed to notice the decree that was handed down to her people. Had she become so callous that she had forgotten her people? Destruction is coming to those who do not believe in the Lord Jesus. Additionally, we live like Esther, not even taking notice. We do not even observe those who are living with fear, anxiety, or complete hopelessness. Many today do not even believe in hell, they only want to believe in Heaven. As we walk through our day, most of us think more about what we are going to eat for dinner than we think about where someone will spend eternity. Most of us rather talk about our favorite sports team or our preferred place to shop than tell someone about Jesus Christ.

POA #2-Are we CASTING our hope in people or God?

Mordecai says to Esther, "Maybe you have been chosen for such a time as this?" Earlier in the book, Mordecai doesn't want Esther to tell of who she was. He had placed all his hope in Esther, now he is CASTING all his hope in God. Mordecai didn't become frantic, he became confident. When God seemed hidden, Mordecai trusted in the one person he knew could save him and his people, God. History had taught him that God keeps his promises. Abraham and Sarah were old, yet God gave them a son. God spared their son when Abraham took him to the altar to be sacrificed. The descendants of Abraham were saved from Egypt when God parted the Red Sea. With genocide looming over the Jews, Mordecai encourages Esther. He knows that God will use her, despite the obstacle of going before a king when not invited. God seems hidden, but He is working. Esther's first inclination was to opt-out. She, just like many of us, make excuses about why it is extremely risky or too disagreeable to get involved in the danger of the world around us. Esther could have chosen to stay behind the walls of the palace but eventually, the decree of Haman would have ruined her as well as her people. We seek safety behind the walls of our home or our church, believing we will not be disturbed by the harshness of this world. But what is outside always finds a way inside, and our initial response is to opt-out. For many of us, we would rather sit in the stands and witness the fight from a distance. But we must get out of the stands, jump into the arena, fight and persevere. We must understand that God is working it all out for us. He is very meticulous and has a place and purpose for each of us. We need to exchange our dreams for His desires, amend our security for the salvation of others. We must serve alongside God, even if it costs us our lives.

POA #3-Knowing God's CHARACTER gives us hope

The Jews were experiencing a significant crisis. Mordecai has pleaded with Esther to go before the king. When we undergo a severe crisis, we can find hope in God by knowing more of His character. Throughout scripture, some others who had faced similar situations. When the giant Goliath taunted the children of Israel, David found hope in God. When Abraham went to sacrifice his son, he equally found hope in God. When we take the time to learn more about who God is, we will learn to trust what he executes. Learn more of God's character, find the hope that will sustain you through the gloomy times.

POA #4-CHOOSING to move roadblocks

One of the biggest roadblocks that can restrict us from moving forward is fear. When Mordecai's words assailed the ears of Esther, fear set in immediately. She identified the danger of going before the king without being asked. The definition of fear is: "a distressing emotion aroused by impending danger, evil, pain, etc. whether the threat is real or imagined." [4]   Three things about fear. First, fear cripples! Fear is not the thing we are frightened of; it is our reaction to that thing. Second, fear confines us! It limits what we observe. Many times fears will forestall us before we even get started. Third, Fear is changeable! It is a barrier, an obstruction not a dead end. You can drive through a roadblock, but not a dead end. Don't give in to your fear. Fear never has to be the end of the road.

POA #5-CONQUER an obstacle one day at a time

Mordecai urges Esther to dig deeper into her soul. He reminds her that the impending death will also strike her as well as her people. The pivotal point in the story rests upon the word Mordecai says, "Maybe you have been chosen for such a time as this." Esther chose to conquer her fear, remove the roadblock. There are times in our lives when we are terrified. There are times when we procrastinate. Many times God summons us to do something for Him, but fear haunts us, cripples us, causes us to not pursue what God has called us to do. The solitary way we can get the courage to achieve what we are supposed to achieve is to conquer one obstacle at a time. Trust in God, trust that He will enable you to overcome each difficulty of life one day at a time.

"When Mordecai learned all that had occurred, he tore his clothes, put on sackcloth and ashes, went into the middle of the city, and cried loudly and bitterly. He only went as far as the King's Gate, since the law prohibited anyone wearing sackcloth from entering the King's Gate. There was great mourning among the Jewish people in every province where the king's command and edict came. They fasted, wept, and lamented, and many lay on sackcloth and ashes. Esther's female servants and her eunuchs came and reported the news to her, and the queen was overcome with fear. She sent clothes for Mordecai to wear so he could take off his sackcloth, but he did not accept them. Esther summoned Hathach, one of the king's eunuchs assigned to her, and dispatched him to Mordecai to learn what he was doing and why. So

Hathach went out to Mordecai in the city square in front of the King's Gate. Mordecai told him everything that had happened as well as the exact amount of money Haman had promised to pay the royal treasury for the slaughter of the Jews. Mordecai also gave him a copy of the written decree issued in Susa ordering their destruction, so that Hathach might show it to Esther, explain it to her, and command her to approach the king, implore his favor, and plead with him personally for her people. Hathach came and repeated Mordecai's response to Esther. Esther spoke to Hathach and commanded him to tell Mordecai, 'All the royal officials and the people of the royal provinces know that one law applies to every man or woman who approaches the king in the inner courtyard and who has not been summoned—the death penalty. Only if the king extends the gold scepter will that person live. I have not been summoned to appear before the king for the last 30 days.' Esther's response was reported to Mordecai. Mordecai told the messenger to reply to Esther. 'Don't think that you will escape the fate of all the Jews because you are in the king's palace. If you keep silent at this time, liberation and deliverance will come to the Jewish people from another place, but you and your father's house will be destroyed. Who knows, perhaps you have come to your royal position for such a time as this.' Esther sent this reply to Mordecai: 'Go and assemble all the Jews who can be found in Susa and fast for me. Don't eat or drink for three days, day or night. I and my female servants will also fast in the same way. After that, I will go to the king even if it is against the law. If I perish, I perish.' So Mordecai went and did everything Esther had ordered him"(Esther 4 HCSB).

Chapter 5-"Exhilarated"
Esther 5

Party Given By Esther-Banquet #6
Esther's 1st Banquet-Cliffhanger #3

My servant comes into my room, he tells me I am wanted by Queen Esther. He escorts me to a private room. As I enter, I note the tension. Esther is looking out a window. She turns to me and says, "I know you are writing everything down, but please write down what you see next. I am going to the king. I am risking my life, I might die." I merely indicate in agreement. One of her servants places her imperial robe on her. She stands tall, vacates the room and heads for the inner court of the king.

As she turns the corner, immediately she sees the king sitting on his throne. She stands there quietly. He glances up and considers her. He holds out his golden scepter, inviting her to approach. She moves forward cautiously, she reaches forward to touch the tip of the scepter. So far, so good. I can tell by the expression on his face; he is delighted to see her. He says, "My dear Queen Esther, what do you desire from me? Submit your request and I will give you whatever you want. I will indeed bequeath you half of my kingdom if that is your desire." She says, "If it pleases the king, I want to invite you and Haman to a dinner party."

"Someone get Haman now," says the king.
Before I realize it, they are enjoying a meal together. While at the table, I hear the king ask again, "Now what is it you require my dear. You know, I will give you whatever you desire."

Esther responds, "What I want, is for you and Haman to come again tomorrow to another dinner party, then I will tell you exactly what I want."

THE PLOT THICKENS

That evening, I summon my servant to find out if I can talk to Esther because I am extremely intrigued about why she is arranging this next dinner.

I am led to the same room as before. I enter, I see Esther standing by a narrow table. I ask, "Queen Esther, I am puzzled about why you didn't tell the king what you desired?"
She answers, "I have a plan. You will see it tomorrow."

I leave nevertheless puzzled. As I am heading back to my room, I see Haman coming down the hall. He doesn't pay much attention to me, so I decided to follow him. I think to myself, *"Wow, he seems thrilled about something."* I continue following him to see where he is going. On his way out, he has to pass by Mordecai again. He pauses when he sees Mordecai, I am certain he is waiting for him to bow. This time, Mordecai completely disregards him. Instantly, Haman is furious. He storms out of the palace and heads to his house.

When he reaches the front yard, there are many friends there, his wife and sons. Right away, Haman starts talking. He says, "I have plenty of money, an extraordinary family and a glorious job. I can't believe the king has made me second in command. Matter of fact, I just came from a dinner party with the king and queen. I'm so excited because I am attending another one tomorrow. But there is one problem, I can't enjoy any of this because of Mordecai. When I look at him, I am furious."

His friends, his wife, and his family start thinking. They say, "We have a brilliant idea. Construct a gallows, build it seventy-five feet high. Then tomorrow morning, go to the king, have him formulate a law to hang Mordecai on it."

Haman says, "That is an excellent idea."

He calls for some carpenters to get started. They work all night building this gallows to hang Mordecai.

POINTS TO CONSIDER

#1-HESITATION OR STRATEGY

As you know, Esther has concealed her identity. The king doesn't know she is a Jew, so when she goes to make her request, we have to wonder if she is being hesitant. Not only does she not make her request, but she also invites the king and Haman to a banquet. To make things worse, when they arrive at this banquet, she puts the king off for another day, inviting him and Haman to another party. You have to wonder what she is up to. Is she frightened? Is she dealing with some hesitation? Is she employing some kind of strategy? I think when you look at the story; she is hesitant based on the fact that she hasn't informed the king of whom she genuinely is. But on the other hand, strategy is fulfilling the more critical role here. Let's consider two possible strategies.

STRATEGY #1-DELAY

In the culture of that day, it was conventional for requests and petitions to be brought forward during a banquet or feast. She invited them to the first meal, not presenting her request, but delaying it, inviting the king and Haman to a second meal. Plus, this probably piques the king's curiosity.

STRATEGY #2-DESIGN

Requiring a more concentrated look, we see Esther recognizes what her plan is and is setting up the pieces on the chessboard. She is pursuing a well-designed plan. By adopting the first strategy of delaying her request, she has directly moved the two crucial players into position by compelling them to come to the next banquet. The king is already perplexed. He is ready and willing to give half of his kingdom and to grant any request. Haman's pride is so evident he has completely let his guard down. Right away she is prepared to commence with her plan.

POINTS OF APPLICATION

POA #1-A CONCEALED God?

When we arrive at this point in the story, we don't recognize God's hand. It seems Haman obtains more control over the fate of God's people than God does.

How often does this sound familiar? How many times does our life follow like the book of Esther? Distressing things happen in life that we do not seem to comprehend. There are times when we think a resolution has arrived only to find out things are considerably worse than we essentially thought. Every so often things seems so incredibly out of control that we wonder where God is in the midst of it. Sometimes things are so wrong we wonder why God has not intervened. Many times we merely don't understand what God is doing. But just like Esther had a plan, so does God, and His plan is greater than we can even imagine. The key is to not formulate any abrupt conclusions about God because He seems hidden behind the massive oak tree in the backyard. In the book of Esther, we see many exceptional banquets or parties. Our lives are permeated with plenty of parties. If one party ends, soon another one will arrive. God is purposefully transforming your disappointments into accomplishments. When you are invited to the banquet table and all you see is chaos, don't give up because another course of outstanding food is ready to be served.

POA #2-A CALL for strategy

Strategies have played a major role so far throughout the book of Esther. Mordecai employed a strategy to make sure Esther didn't tell of her background placing her in the precise place to become queen. Another strategy has come into play as Esther is designing a plan to save her people. So what about us? To begin with, strategies have been downplayed in the minds of most Christians. The Bible says, *"Many are the plans in a person's heart, but it is the LORD"s purpose that prevails."* When that verse of scripture has been taught, many have believed that if we come up with a plan of our own then we are going against God. This belief is a fallacy. We must live our life with a purpose and a plan. If we are trying to serve God in the capacity of what He has called us to do with no plan, then we have become irresponsible. Having a purpose is the " WHAT" that drives us, a strategy is the "HOW!" But to advance that strategy into action we must do as Esther did. We must spend some time in prayer.

POA #3-A COMMAND for priorities

Haman leaves the banquet with his head held aloft, his chest puffed out. But as soon as he sees Mordecai, his exaltation turns to indignation. As soon as Haman arrives at his house, he is bragging about his wealth, his sons, and his invitations to two private banquets with the king and queen. But he notifies his friends and his wife that he can't be cheerful because of Mordecai. His wife urges him to build a 75-foot gallows to hang Mordecai on. By all rights, Haman looked like a successful man. He enjoys an enormous family, a padded bank account, and he is second in command to the king. Moreover, he is miserable because of one man, Mordecai. This brings us to take a closer look at ourselves. What makes us really happy? What makes us angry or unhappy? We may not like the answer we give, but we can merely become the person God wants us to be when we put our priorities in order. We must identify what makes us happy or unhappy.

"On the third day, Esther dressed up in her royal clothing and stood in the inner courtyard of the palace facing it. The king was sitting on his royal throne in the royal courtroom, facing its entrance. As soon as the king saw Queen Esther standing in the courtyard, she won his approval. The king extended the gold scepter in his hand toward Esther, and she approached and touched the tip of the scepter. 'What is it, Queen Esther?' the king asked her. 'Whatever you want, even to half the kingdom, will be given to you.' 'If it pleases the king,' Esther replied, 'may the king and Haman come today to the banquet I have prepared for them.' The king commanded, 'Hurry, and get Haman so we can do as Esther has requested.' So the king and Haman went to the banquet Esther had prepared.

While drinking the wine, the king asked Esther, 'Whatever you ask will be given to you. Whatever you want, even to half the kingdom, will be done.' Esther answered, 'This is my petition and my request: If the king approves of me and if it pleases the king to grant my petition and perform my request, may the king and Haman come to the banquet I will prepare for them. Tomorrow I will do what the king has asked.' That day Haman left full of joy and in good spirits. But when Haman saw Mordecai at the King's Gate, and Mordecai didn't rise or tremble in fear at his presence, Haman was filled with rage toward Mordecai. Yet Haman controlled himself and went home. He sent for his friends and his wife Zeresh to join him. Then Haman described for them his glorious wealth and his many sons. He told them all how the king had honored him and promoted him in rank over the other officials and the royal staff. 'What's more,' Haman added, 'Queen Esther invited no one but me to join the king at the banquet she had prepared. I am invited again tomorrow to join her with the king. Still, none of this satisfies me since I see Mordecai the Jew sitting at the King's Gate all the time.' His wife Zeresh and all his friends told him, 'Have them build a gallows 75 feet high. Ask the king in the morning to hang Mordecai on it. Then go to the banquet with the king and enjoy yourself.' The advice pleased Haman, so he had the gallows constructed"(Esther 5 HCSB).

Chapter 6 - "Humiliated"
Esther 6

PALACE HUMILIATION

At the exact same moment the gallows was being built, the king was unable to sleep. He calls for some attendants, he urges them to bring some history books to read. I am awakened by my servant because the king wants to make sure I don't overlook anything. As I enter the king's quarters with my servant, I petition the king, "What seems to be bothering you?" He replies, "I don't know for sure, so I am going to have these history books read to me, maybe they will be so boring, I will fall asleep."

I sit there listening to the reading of these books. A few hours have passed by, I observe daylight arriving. About that time, they get to the part of Mordecai spoiling the plot to slay the king. This recorded story caught his attention and so he asks, "What honor has been bestowed upon Mordecai for him saving my life?" "Nothing has been done for him," says an attendant.

The king jumps out of bed. He says, "I will execute this as my first action of the day." The king, furthermore, asks, "Who is in the court?" Most mornings the court is empty, but on this particular morning, there was someone there. The attendant looks out into the court and says, "Haman is here, he is standing in the court." "Permit him to come in," the king replies.

The king is excited because Haman is there, but he doesn't know the reason why. Haman is equally excited because he can't believe the king is already awake and wanting to see him. Haman walks in, ready to spew out the words that he has planned out in his head. But before Haman can announce anything, the king asks,

"What should be done to the man in whom the king delights to honor?"

Haman is amazed because naturally, he thinks the king is referring to him. Consequently, he thinks to himself, *"He must be talking about me, who else?"* Haman responds by saying, "Bring a royal robe that the king has worn and a horse that the king has ridden, one with a royal crown on its head. In addition, give the robe and the horse to one of the king's most noble princes. Have him robe the man whom the king wants to honor; have the prince lead him on horseback through the city square, proclaiming before him, 'This is what is done for the man whom the king especially wants to honor!'"

The king says to Haman, "Go and implement what you have stated, do it quickly. Gather the robe and horse and honor Mordecai, do not leave any detail out."

PARADE HUMILIATION

As Haman gets everything prepared, people in the city square are anticipating a sensational event. I make my way to the square to watch. I see Mordecai upon a horse, donning a royal robe, being led through the streets. Haman is shouting over and over, "This is what is done for the man whom the king especially wants to honor!"

After the parade, Mordecai returns back to his job at the king's gate. Haman covers his head and his face. He is mortified at the events that have just occurred. He hurries to his house, describes to his wife everything. She doesn't give him any support. She says, "If Mordecai is a Jew, you don't stand a chance. You will inevitably fall." While they were talking the king's eunuchs arrived and took Haman to have dinner with the king and Queen Esther.

POINTS TO CONSIDER

#1-INCREDIBLE EVENTS
When we take the time to pause for a moment and look at the events that have just transpired, we can see they are incredible. It would also cause many of us to believe these events were merely coincidental. How many times have we said, "That had to be a coincidence", for events that have taken place in our lives? This causes us to wonder if there is such a thing as coincidences. If we examine the dictionary, we see the word "coincidence" is defined as, *"a remarkable concurrence of events or circumstances without apparent causal connection."* In other words, something rare happens without anyone making it happen.

Notice how things play out in Esther 6. The king can't sleep, so he starts reading. He comes to a part about how Mordecai saved his life. Mordecai's is in danger of being killed by Haman who happens to arrive at that exact moment. Incredible? Definitely! Coincidental? Possibly!

#2-IRONY OF REVERSAL
Haman is having a gallows built all night long to hang Mordecai. While the king was reading about Mordecai, Haman walks into the court wanting to tell the king about Mordecai and the gallows. Naturally, Haman is only thinking of himself. He lives in an artificial reality. Haman is a genuine narcissist. Haman is daydreaming, so when the king mentions Mordecai is to be honored, Haman's greatest dream becomes his most dreadful nightmare. It's at this precise moment; a significant reversal has occurred. This is additionally a key turning point in the book of Esther.

#3-INFLUENCE

Even though the book of Esther is titled after her, she is not spoken about much in the book. In this chapter, we hear mostly of Haman and the king. But look at the responses of Mordecai and Haman. After Mordecai was honored, he had every chance in the world to rub it in the face of Haman, but he didn't. He just went back to the king's gate to perform his job. At this point in the story, Esther has been in the palace for many years as the queen. She has seen many different things. She has learned how to be in the Persian government, she has learned politics, yet her character still shows the signs of humility. Clearly, she has been influenced by Mordecai. He demonstrates great humility while being honored, therefore, we believe through her years growing up under Mordecai it has molded her character.

POINTS OF APPLICATION

POA #1-COINCIDENCE

Do you believe in coincidence? I believe at certain times we all believe in it. There is only one place in scripture where we uncover what we would consider a coincidence. Jesus, Himself voiced the word when He told the parable of the Good Samaritan. When you look at the Greek translation of the word coincidence, it is derived from two words, "sun" and "kurios." "Sun" meaning, "together with" and "Kurios" meaning, "authority."Which leaves us with a biblical definition such as: "what occurs simultaneously by God's providential arrangement of circumstances. Esther 6 provides us with some of the most extraordinary coincidences we have ever seen. Yet, all the while, God was orchestrating His plan. The same goes for all of us.

We have a tendency to believe there is no coincidence when it comes to the more substantial things in our lives, but when it comes to the smaller things we inherently believe in coincidences. Often times, God seems silent, for we do not observe the working of His Almighty Hand, but when we read this story in Esther it proves to us that God is working for us. There are times when He breaks into our stories with miracles and unexplainable events. At other times, He clearly allows certain pieces to fall into place.

POA #2-CONNECTIONS of influence

Most of us want to believe that Esther or Mordecai was the a genuine hero in the book of Esther. But the hero is God. We do not hear His name mentioned or even read His name in the book, but He is working behind the scenes. Two people in Esther's life had a profound influence on her. God and Mordecai. Certain events equally had a significant influence on Esther. Often times those who influence us the most are those that are silent. Who influences your life? God? A co-worker, pastor, teacher, mother, or father? Take a short moment today and think of someone who has a profound influence on your life.

POA #3-The CARDS

Within the story of Esther, it seems that Mordecai has been forgotten. It seems that everything has gone terribly wrong. But behind the scenes, God is working. God holds all the cards. God knows the future. Therefore He knows exactly the right time to play the right card. How about you? Are you having a troublesome time seeing what God is doing in your life? Are you wondering where God is? Is He hiding behind the big oak tree? God is holding all the cards for you. Conceivably you are thinking He should have already played a certain card for you. Here is the problem for most of us. Typically we don't mind trusting God especially if we see Him working for us. But as soon as things go south for us, when things seem extremely undesirable, when we are desperate and do not understand, we end up trying to figure things out on our own. Every so often we indeed ask others what they presume. Every so often we do not get the answer we are anticipating. Periodically we don't agree with the answer so we find ourselves living in fear and paralysis and it prevents us from moving forward. Remember this, we at times may search out help from our pastor, friends, or family, and they might not have the answer either. Harsh things will look really bad. But grasp this: God provides a plan for your story, and He holds all the cards. He will play the right card at the right time. You might not quite comprehend it at that moment, but eventually, you will.

"That night sleep escaped the king, so he ordered the book recording daily events to be brought and read to the king. They found the written report of how Mordecai had informed on Bigthana and Teresh, two eunuchs who guarded the king's entrance, when they planned to assassinate King Ahasuerus. The king inquired, "What honor and special recognition have been given to Mordecai for this act?" The king's personal attendants replied, "Nothing has been done for him." The king asked, "Who is in the court?" Now Haman was just entering the outer court of the palace to ask the king to hang Mordecai on the gallows he had prepared for him. The king's attendants answered him, "Haman is there, standing in the court." "Have

him enter," the king ordered. Haman entered, and the king asked him, "What should be done for the man the king wants to honor?" Haman thought to himself, "Who is it the king would want to honor more than me?" Haman told the king, "For the man the king wants to honor: Have them bring a royal garment that the king himself has worn and a horse the king himself has ridden, which has a royal diadem on its head. Put the garment and the horse under the charge of one of the king's most noble officials. Have them clothe the man the king wants to honor, parade him on the horse through the city square, and proclaim before him, 'This is what is done for the man the king wants to honor.'" The king told Haman, "Hurry, and do just as you proposed. Take a garment and a horse for Mordecai the Jew, who is sitting at the King's Gate. Do not leave out anything you have suggested." So Haman took the garment and the horse. He clothed Mordecai and paraded him through the city square, crying out before him, "This is what is done for the man the king wants to honor." Then Mordecai returned to the King's Gate, but Haman, overwhelmed, hurried off for home with his head covered. Haman told his wife Zeresh and all his friends everything that had happened. His advisers and his wife Zeresh said to him, "Since Mordecai is Jewish, and you have begun to fall before him, you won't overcome him, because your downfall is certain." While they were still speaking with him, the eunuchs of the king arrived and rushed Haman to the banquet Esther had prepared" (Esther 6 HCSB).

CHAPTER 7 - "HANGED"
ESTHER 7

PLOT IS SPOILED
PARTY GIVEN BY ESTHER - BANQUET #7
ESTHER'S 2nd BANQUET

I am sitting not too far away from the banquet, Haman, the king, and Esther are all sitting around the table. Thick tension is in the air. Esther knows it is time to "spill the beans." For five years she has withheld her identity from the king. Presently she is nervous, and wondering how he is going to react to her surprising secret. To help us gain an understanding of how Esther is feeling at the moment, allow me to tell you a story about the kind of man Esther is married to.

Looking back into the history books, I noticed a story about the king. A man had given King Ahasuerus an enormous sum of money to fight against the Greeks. This man had five sons who were serving in the army. The king and this certain individual seemed to be reasonably good friends. They had even been invited to each other's houses on significant occasions. This man wanted to pass on his family name through one of his sons, so he petitioned the king to see if he would release the eldest son from his military duty. After all, he didn't believe it was too much to ask considering the sizeable gift he had presented to the king. The king seized the eldest son; the one in which the father wanted to be released, cut him in half with a sword. Next, he had his army walk in between the two halves of this young man's body.

This is the man whom she is about to divulge her secret to and submit a certain request. As they were partaking of their meal, I am sure Esther kept repeating her plea inside her head, adjusting it to make it sound better. I am sitting there wondering when she is going to present her request to the king.

I am not completely sure what the king is feeling at the moment. I witness the king and Haman engaging in foolish talk. After a few moments, I hear the king once again inquire of Esther, "What is your request? Half of my kingdom? Merely ask and it is yours."
Esther says, "If I have obtained favor in your eyes, O King, give me my life and the lives of my people. We have been sold to be destroyed and eliminated. I would have kept silent, our troubles are not worth burdening the king."

I watch as the king, jumps up from the table, knocking over a few chairs. He explodes in anger, shouting, "Who? Where is he? Who is the man that would dare carry out such a thing?" I watch as I see the king's face turn brilliant red, but I can equally see he is puzzled. Simultaneously, he doesn't even recognize who he is supposed to be angry at.

I look over at Haman. His face is just as red as the kings. As Haman is trying to regain his breath, all of a sudden he hears Esther say, "The adversary, this enemy, is the EVIL Haman." At this point Haman is terrified. The look in his eyes speaks volumes.

PITFALL OF HAMAN

My attention is on Haman, but I see the king full of rage, walk away from the table out into the garden. At that moment, Haman doesn't grasp what to put together. If he runs after the king, that would spell disaster considering the state of mind the king is in right now. If he runs off to hide, that will only just make him look guilty. Therefore what does he do? He runs to the other side of the table, falls to the floor on his knees, pleading with Queen Esther. (By the way, technically it is against protocol for a man to be within seven steps of the queen or even speak to her without the king being there.) The king is furiously pacing in the garden. He is trying to think of what he should do. The king walks back into the banquet hall, sees Haman groveling at the feet of the queen. The king yells out, "You contain enough nerve to molest the queen while I am outside?" As soon as the question was asked, Haman turned completely white.

Right after, the king's eunuch, Harbona said, "Look over there! The gallows that was intended for Mordecai is in Haman's yard, seventy-five feet high. Mordecai saved the king's life."
The king said, "Hang Haman on it!" Two guards came and took Haman away. They escorted him to the gallows and he was hanged at that very moment. As soon as this was accomplished, the king's anger dissipated.

POINTS TO CONSIDER

#1-PRIDE OF HAMAN
If you ever want to undertake a deep study on "pride" then one must study the life of Haman. Let's take some time to consider some key points.
Haman was elevated to the second-most influential person in the Persian empire. He commanded everyone to bow down to him. Moredcai refuses to bow down. Because this was unacceptable by Haman, his pride was so hurt, that instead of just wanting to kill Mordecai, he decided to kill a whole nation. So, how does pride act? Pride is the centerpiece, therefore, it exploits other people to build itself up. Haman believed he was the center attraction. So, how does pride act? It makes us

the centerpiece, therefore it uses people for our benefit.

#2-PATHOGENS

Both of these pathogens or viruses lead to one critical illness. That illness is PRIDE!

Pathogen #1

Many times when Esther is taught or when it is preached from the pulpit, we tend to put a "Snow White" or "Sleeping Beauty" spin on it. We tend to teach about a tale of a majestic king seeking genuine love. However, a more thorough look reveals a violent, prideful king who sexually exploits the women of his kingdom. Think about it for a moment. It was a mass abduction and sexual violation of hundreds of young virgin women. These women, Esther included, are seized, taken from their homes to the capital city. They are prepared for twelve months with makeup in order to "make up" for any flaws they might have. Next, they are forced to spend a night in the king's bed. These women remain objects for the king. The book of Esther speaks clearly for the numerous victims of objectification and exploitation today. The curtain has been pulled back showing the well-kept secrets of this ancient and shameful practice of treating women as things used for personal pleasure. When we leaf through the book of Esther, we must hear the voices of today's endless victims of sex trafficking, domestic abuse, rape, and incest. In the book of Esther, we do not find the "MeToo" movement, which might have supplied them a voice. They all suffered in silence. But as we look at the story, we see God working in the wretched turmoil, raising Esther to a place where she could ultimately transform the culture.

Pathogen #2

Haman is promoted, he then is offended by Mordecai, causing him to hate Mordecai. Haman's pride causes him to come up with a plan to exterminate all the Jews. When we follow the book of Esther, we note how racism and hatred target one individual. It spirals downward toward an entire population. When we allow the sin of pride to be aimed at one person due to their race, class, gender, or orientation, that one seed will blossom into an immeasurable crop.

These pathogens seem disconnected, but they cause the same illness: Pride

Pride of the king: His pride was so inflated that when Queen Vashti refused to parade in front of everyone in the palace, he tossed her out. He then, gathered all young virgins, violating them, leaving them unfit for marriages of their own.

Pride of Haman: Haman's pride was so inflated that when Mordecai refused to bow down before him, he not merely sought to kill Mordecai, but sought out to exterminate a whole race.

Pope Gregory 1 believed that pride was the root cause of all other sins plaguing the human race. He indeed believed pride gave birth to the seven deadly sins. If the seven deadly sins comprise branches on a tree, pride would be the root of that tree.

#3-POWER OF RESPONSIBILITY

When Esther points to Haman as the culprit, the king is infuriated. When the king sees Haman at the feet of the queen, the king loses it. Haman is immediately hung on the gallows. But the interesting fact is the king takes no credit in making the edict to eradicate the Jews. Was he feeling liable, when he ran out into the garden? Did he assume any guilt? The truth is the king took no responsibility at all for his part in the plot. He shoved all the blame on Haman. This might work for a king but not for a tremendous leader. To be an exceptional leader, we must be able to take responsibility. As we have seen, this king was a puppet, being led around by his counselors. Then as soon as something was wrong, he didn't have to take responsibility he could dump it off on someone else. The truth is this: You cannot lead if you do not take responsibility.

#4-POWER OF COURAGE

On the other side of the coin, we encounter Esther. She chose courage. The king has not called for his queen for thirty days. Therefore when she enters the view of the king, she is not in view of an affectionate husband. She is eye-to-eye with an unpredictable tyrant who is likely to sign her death warrant, given his behavior toward the previous queen. Esther selects courage over convenience. She chooses to risk her life rather than sitting on the sideline.

POINTS OF APPLICATION

POA #1-PRIDE

In the book of Esther, Haman is so centered on himself that his pride steers him to the point of wanting to slaughter millions of people. This is what pride does it makes us the center, and it uses people for our benefit. I am certain that neither you or I have tried to kill millions of people, but I am sure we have used people to make ourselves look or feel better. How many times have we looked down on someone else? One author says this, "Most of us probably look down on arrogant people, not realizing that in doing so we are revealing our own form of pride." [5]

How many times have we criticized someone and used their failures to make us feel better about ourselves? How many times have we talked about someone else's problems or about their sin because it made us feel better about ourselves? How many times have we demanded people to listen to our problems or stories, but we disregard them when they begin to tell of their problems?

Since pride causes us to be self-absorbed we need to look at two different forms of it. Pride shows us having a SUPERIOR STATUS and there is pride which shows us having an INFERIOR STATUS. We all grasp what it means to be superior, so let's look at the inferior status. Most of us would have a tendency to believe that being inferior is a sign of humility, but it categorically isn't. It still presents us with the idea that it is all about us, and it still uses people. Instead of rejoicing with other people when they succeed, we focus on our failures. For example, someone plays ping-pong better than us, we just dwell on how much better they are than we are. When we mess up, we only think about how terrible we are. When our best friend is much more talented in singing, or art, or sports, all we do is remind them of how bad we are in all these things. This is just another way that pride causes us to make everything about ourselves.

We need to be humble. Humility recognizes that we are not the center and life isn't about us. It definitely is not about how good we are, or how horrible we are. WE ARE NOT THE CENTER. Humility is best described by C.S. Lewis. He said, "the state of mind where someone could build the best cathedral in the world, and know it was the best, and rejoice in it being the best without being any more or less or otherwise glad at having built it than if someone else had built it." [6]

Tim Kellar says, "Humility isn't thinking less about yourself; but it's thinking about yourself less." [7]
Pride wants to destroy the world, and humility is what will salvage it. This is another message we discover in the book of Esther, this is a message that we equally see in Jesus.

"Do nothing out of selfish ambition or vain conceit. Rather, in humility value others above yourselves, not looking to your own interests but each of you to the interests of the others. In your relationships with one another, have the same mindset as Christ Jesus: Who, being in very nature God, did not consider equality with God something to be used to his own advantage; rather, he made himself nothing by taking the very nature of a servant, being made in human likeness. And being found in appearance as a man, he humbled himself by becoming obedient to death—even death on a cross (Philippians 2:3-8 NIV)!

Jesus' humility rescued the world. Esther's humility rescued a nation.

POA #2-POWER of insane courage

Throughout the book of Esther, we indeed do not hear much about her. We know she was chosen queen, suddenly she becomes silent. Until her people are in danger. At that point, Mordecai pleads with her to go before the king and make a request to deliver her people. She has to gather courage to carry out such a thing and she did. One author said it like this, "All we need is twenty seconds of insane courage. That is the amount of time it would take for Esther to break the traditions, enter the king's presence and risk her life, to instigate a plan to overthrow Haman and rescue her people. It took some time to devise the plan, but it only took twenty seconds to boost the plan off the launch pad."[8]

In 2011, there was a movie titled, "We Bout A Zoo." It tells the true story of Benjamin Mee, played by Matt Daman. In one scene, Damon (Mee) was sitting with his son on some concrete right outside the cages for the tigers. The son, Dylan Mee, played by Colin Ford, is talking about a girl he likes. He says, 'It's like you embarrass yourself if you say something and you embarrass yourself if you don't.' Mee chuckles and says, 'You know sometimes all you need is twenty seconds of insane courage. Just literally twenty seconds of embarrassing bravery. And I promise you, something great will come of it.'" [9]

All of us need twenty seconds of insane courage. But Esther's twenty seconds of insane courage came out of 259,200 seconds of prayer and fasting. Before Esther stepped into the throne room of the Persian king, she stepped into the throne room of her heavenly King. The reason she had the courage to confront the one who wanted to take her life was because she had spent three days praying to the one who had given her life.

Esther and countless other women were victims of government-sanctioned sexual abuse. Her people were targets of unfathomable racism. But Esther's first move was not invasion but invocation. She took a swift step not to punish those abusing power but instead she called for all to pray.

As I am writing this chapter, we are experiencing continued racism in our country. Our hearts are aching as we witness an innocent man being murdered by a police officer. We hear stories of police officers gunned down in cold blood. We watch on television as these events unfold, causing mass rioting in the streets of our beloved cities. We suffer the pain of division in our country. It is time for God's people to follow the lead of Esther. It is time for the church to fall on our knees with fasting and prayer for God to put an end to these evils and to use us as He will.

"The king and Haman came to feast with Esther the queen. Once again, on the second day while drinking wine, the king asked Esther, "Queen Esther, whatever you ask will be given to you. Whatever you seek, even to half the kingdom, will be done." Queen Esther answered, 'If I have obtained your approval, my king, and if the king is pleased, spare my life—this is my request; and spare my people—this is my desire. For my people and I have been sold out to destruction, death, and extermination. If we had merely been sold as male and female slaves, I would have kept silent. Indeed, the trouble wouldn't be worth burdening the king.' King Ahasuerus spoke up and asked Queen Esther, 'Who is this, and where is the one who would devise such a scheme?' Esther answered, "The adversary and enemy is this evil Haman."
Haman stood terrified before the king and queen. Angered by this, the king arose from where they were drinking wine and went to the palace garden. Haman remained to beg Queen Esther for his life because he realized the king was planning something terrible for him. Just as the king returned from the palace garden to the house of wine drinking, Haman was falling on the couch where Esther was reclining. The king exclaimed, 'Would he actually violate the queen while I am in the palace?" As soon as the statement left the king's mouth, Haman's face was

*covered. Harbona, one of the royal eunuchs, said:
"There is a gallows 75 feet tall at Haman's house that
he made for Mordecai, who gave the report that
saved the king.' The king commanded, 'Hang him on
it.' They hanged Haman on the gallows he had
prepared for Mordecai. Then the king's anger
subsided" (Esther 7 HCSB).*

Chapter 8 - "Countered"
Esther 8

PUTTING IN MORDECAI

As I was sitting in my room, writing down some of the events I had just witnessed, I was summoned by the king to come and hear the request of Esther. We were meeting in a room not to far off from the throne room. Mordecai, Esther, and the king were in attendance. Mordecai is there because Esther informed the king who he was to her.

Sitting there I witnessed as the king took off his signet ring, which he had gotten back from Haman and handed it to Mordecai. He in addition gave Esther the house of Haman. The king had actually tried forgetting the edict that was still in effect to kill all of the Jews. He was likely hoping that Esther would have forgotten as well. He was hoping that she would just go about her duties as queen. Instead, she fell to his feet.

PLEADING FOR DELIVERANCE

Esther wept and pleaded with the king to avert the evil plan that Haman had initiated. The king extended his golden scepter toward Esther. She got up and stood before the king. I was listening intently to observe what her request would be. Esther said, "If it pleases you O king, and if I have obtained approval before you, if the matter seems right to you, if I am pleasing in your sight, then let a royal decree be written. Let the decree of Haman be revoked, let the documents of the destroying of the Jews be destroyed. I cannot bear to see this disaster come upon my people. I will be unable to bear the destruction of my relatives."

PROCLAMATION OF MORDECAI

I could hear the pleading in her voice. The king looked at Esther and Mordecai then he said, "Look, I have transferred Haman's estate to Esther, therefore, you can write in the king's name whatever pleases you concerning the Jews. You may seal it with the royal signet ring. For as you know, a document written in the king's name and sealed with the royal signet ring cannot be revoked."

The royal scribes were then called for. This was on the 23rd day of the third month. They wrote down everything that Mordecai ordered for them to write down concerning the Jews. The order was written and disbursed to each province in its own writing, for each ethnic group in their own language, and to the Jews in their own writing and language.

The order was laid out on the table in front of us. I watched as Mordecai wrote in the king's name and sealed it with the royal signet ring. The documents were sent out by couriers on the swiftest horses.

They handed me a copy of the decree, so I could read it for myself. I noticed that each Jew in each and every city will retain the right to assemble and defend themselves. They will be able to destroy, kill, and annihilate every ethnic and provincial army that is hostile to them, including women and children. They will also be allowed to seize their possessions as the plunder of war. This will all take place on a solitary day, the thirteenth day of the twelfth month.

PRESTIGE GIVEN-BANQUET #8

Moredecai was immediately dressed in clothing of purple and white. I watched as the king placed a gold crown on the head of Mordecai, and a purple robe was draped around him. Mordecai walked out of the palace and into the streets of the city of Susa. Everywhere he went the Jews shouted with great rejoicing and bestowed supreme honor to Mordecai. Many of the ethnic groups started proclaiming themselves as Jews for they were afraid the Jews would overcome them.

As I made my way back to my sleeping quarters, I thought about all of the events that had taken place. I thought to myself, *"What a significant turn of events."*

POINTS TO CONSIDER

#1-ANNIHILATION

One of the most catastrophic events that I can remember hearing about is that of the Rwanda genocide. For 100 days many lives were slaughtered in the year 1994. Most of the Hutu's and Tutsi's had been civil to each other and some of them had even become friends. But in 1994 the President of the Hutus was killed when his plane was shot down. A meticulous organizing of slaughter had ensued. Neighbors were killing neighbors. Husbands were killing their Tutsi wives. The total annihilation of the Tutsi's was the order handed down by the government to extremist groups. By the time the 100-day slaughter had ended over 800,000 Tutsi's were killed. Can you imagine what it must have been like to be a Tutsi in Rwanda during that time? Wondering if your next-door neighbors would enter and slay you? Why, would I bring up such a horrifying event? Because it aids us in understanding what was going on during the time of Esther.

Straightforward instructions had been issued by Persia to eradicate all of the Jews. Young, old, women and children to be totally annihilated on the thirteenth day of the twelfth month. If you were a Jew living in that day and you had read the decree handed out by the king and Haman, how difficult it must have been to be living next door to someone of Persia or working alongside with one every day. Everywhere you went, you were stared at. Those you have made friends with were suddenly not talking to you. Next door neighbors arguing about who is going to collect your stuff after you are slain. The Jews had no escape.

We hear stories like the one in Persia, or you read a story about those who lost their lives in Rwanda, and we think it could never happen to us. But like I have already said, I am writing this during an evening when the news is filled with so much racial tension and unrest in our country. Will we ever get to the point such as we have read above? I pray and hope that we don't.

#2-APPEASED/ASSUMES

Esther had gone before the king making her request known. Haman was the culprit and on the evening of her request, he was hung on his own gallows. After his death, all of Haman's stuff was given to Esther. This seemed to appease the king. Mordecai was given Haman's position as the second most powerful man in the empire. The king returns to his throne believing everything had been settled. The king had saved the life of Esther and her family. He had given Mordecai a powerful position. The king assumes that all is well with Esther and he immediately forgets about the decree that is in effect.

PERSONAL APPLICATIONS

POA #1-CONSUME

If you are a Christian, you have been spared from hell. Yet, there is a day approaching when God will judge all of His enemies and those who have rejected Him.

Jonathan Edwards describes hell like this: *"The devils in hell will hate all of the damned souls there. They hated them while in this world and that is why they sought their ruin through their subtle temptations. They thirsted for the blood of their souls, because they hated them; they longed to get them in their power to torment them; they watched them as a roaring lion does his prey; because they hated them, therefore they flew upon their souls like hell-hounds, as soon as ever they were parted from their bodies, full of eagerness to torment them. And now that they have them in their power they will spend eternity in tormenting them with the utmost strength and cruelty that devils are capable of. They are as it were, continually and eternally tearing these poor damned souls that are in their hands. And these souls will not only be hated and tormented by devils but they will have no love or pity toward one another, and will be like devils one to another, and will, to their utmost, torment each other, being like brands in the fire, each of which helps to burn the others."* [10]

Esther had spared her family and nation from devastation. We have been spared by Jesus Christ from eternal damnation. Many of us have chosen to place our trust in Jesus, and we have been delivered from the torment of hell we have just read about. But now let us consider how we have responded to the good news. I believe that for many of us we have responded the way the king wanted Esther to respond. The king went right back to his throne. He was hoping and believing that Esther would go back to her duties as queen. He was hoping Mordecai would return to the king's gate and continue to perform his job.

For many of us, after knowing we are spared from the eternal fire of hell go back to focusing on our jobs and our families. For many of us, we have returned to pursuing comfort and pleasure while the people around us are still living under the threat of judgment. Therefore let's consider for a moment about the things that consume us? In other words, what are we investing our lives in? Work? Family? Worrying about what others think about us? Are we thinking about the weekend and how we are going to spend it? What consumes our thoughts each day? What captures our attention throughout our day?

What if Esther had allowed other things to consume her thoughts? She presently possesses Haman's house. What if she had gone to the Persian Home Depot and bought paint to start redecorating the house, so she could rent it out? What if she decided to go on vacation to relieve herself from the stress she has endured over the last few weeks? What if she decided to go back to her job performing the duties of the queen?

I know those thoughts seem crazy, unreal, and absurd. But what if she merely forgot about the decree? Millions of Jews are out there knowing that death is coming. What if she decided not to worry about them now that her life has been spared?

POA #2-CURSE

Esther begins explaining to the king why she just can't ignore the decree, knowing her people are still under the curse of death. Therefore, she pleads with him by falling on her face before him. She tells him she can't bear to see them destroyed. She can't focus on herself, knowing the day is coming when they will be utterly tormented and destroyed.

In 2018, 64 firefighters died in America by saving the lives of others. [11] *In 2018 there were over 144 police officers in America who died in the line of duty.* [12] *On September 11, 2001, there were over 412 emergency workers who died at the foot of the twin towers.* [13]

These men and women risk their lives to save people whose lives are in danger. They can't bear watching a life be destroyed without doing something about it. This should cause us to stop and think about the lives of people living around us. If an officer, a firefighter or a paramedic, are willing to save the physical life of a person, how much more should we be willing to try and save a life from spiritual danger? Over and over again, we go through life thinking only of ourselves, our jobs, our pleasures, while people all around us are perishing. We contain the message of hope they so desperately need.

Men and women are spiritually cursed. There is a decree given that will ultimately be fulfilled. Esther took the time to go before the king to plead for her people. You and I have been saved from death because Jesus went to plead before God on our behalf. Shouldn't we go before our heavenly King and plead for those who are headed down the pathway to hell? Don't you think we should remain people who refuses to live for ourselves as long as there are people going to hell?

As I formulate these words, I am prompted by how many times I do not plead with God for the souls of my family and friends. Forgive me, Lord, for my lack of care. We all possess the privilege of receiving the good news of Jesus Christ. The question presently is, "What are we going to do with it?"

If you are a Christian and you are reading this book, you have been liberated from the torments of hell because someone shared with you the gospel of Jesus Christ. How much more should we be willing to share with those we know are currently on their way to eternal suffering? Many times we like to quote Romans 10:13 which is given at the end of the following paragraph, but we forget about verse 14. Look at what it states. *"How, then, can they call on the one they have not believed in? And how can they believe in the one of whom they have not heard? And how can they hear without someone preaching to them"(Romans 10:14 NIV)?*

If you are not a Christian and you have made it this far into the book. I want you to know that you can be free. I desire you to know the height and depth and breadth of Jesus' love for you. Today, I pray you will come to know the ONE whose name is Jesus. He came and died on the cross for your sins. He arose three days later so that you can obtain forgiveness for your sins. This very day, repent of those sins and place your absolute trust in Him so that you will experience the joy and gladness that comes from encountering Jesus' love. The Bible says, *"Everyone who calls on the name of the Lord will be saved" (Romans 10:13 NIV).*

POA #3-CHOSEN

After Haman's death, the king executed the only thing he knows what to do, he immediately turns over his responsibilities to others. He gives his signet ring to Mordecai. After the queen pleads for her people, the king turns over the task of changing the decree to the queen and Mordecai. We immediately feel some disappointment with the king, but at least he has given the power to the right people this time. At the end of Chapter 8, it is fascinating to see that many have decided to associate with the Jews because of fear. A significant reversal has once again happened. The same people who avoided the Jews out of fear are not joining them for safety. But this demonstrates to us how God is at work. This is another time when we can behold God working when we don't believe we see Him at all. All Christians will go through this life facing some type of trial. We might even face loss or abandonment in our lives. But grasp this; God wants to take your trouble and redeem it. He wants to take your pain and transform it into an opportunity. Esther had been chosen for a reason. She hid her background, her ethnicity, but God capitalized on it for a mighty purpose. You and I are chosen for a reason, and oftentimes, that reason has to do with God bringing well into the world out of the things we hide. God utilizes every part of our story for His glory.

"That same day King Ahasuerus awarded Queen Esther the estate of Haman, the enemy of the Jews. Mordecai entered the king's presence because Esther had revealed her relationship to Mordecai. The king removed his signet ring he had recovered from Haman and gave it to Mordecai, and Esther put him in charge of Haman's estate. Then Esther addressed the king again. She fell at his feet, wept, and begged him to revoke the evil of Haman the Agagite, and his plot he had devised against the Jews. The king extended the gold scepter toward Esther, so she got up and stood before the king. She said, "If it pleases the king, and I have found approval before him, if the matter seems right to the king and I am pleasing in his sight, let a royal edict be written. Let it revoke the

documents the scheming Haman son of Hammedatha the Agagite, wrote to destroy the Jews who are in all the king's provinces. For how could I bear to see the disaster that would come on my people? How could I bear to see the destruction of my relatives?" King Ahasuerus said to Esther the Queen and to Mordecai the Jew, "Look, I have given Haman's estate to Esther, and he was hanged on the gallows because he attacked the Jews. You may write in the king's name whatever pleases you concerning the Jews, and seal it with the royal signet ring. A document written in the king's name and sealed with the royal signet ring cannot be revoked." On the twenty-third day of the third month (that is, the month Sivan), the royal scribes were summoned. Everything was written exactly as Mordecai ordered for the Jews, to the satraps, the governors, and the officials of the 127 provinces from India to Cush. The edict was written for each province in its own script, for each ethnic group in its own language, and to the Jews in their own script and language. Mordecai wrote in King Ahasuerus's name and sealed the edicts with the royal signet ring. He sent the documents by mounted couriers, who rode fast horses bred from the royal racing mares.The king's edict gave the Jews in each and every city the right to assemble and defend themselves, to destroy, kill, and annihilate every ethnic and provincial army hostile to them, including women and children, and to take their possessions as spoils of war. This would take place on a single day throughout all the provinces of King Ahasuerus, on the thirteenth day of the twelfth month, the month Adar.

A copy of the text, issued as law throughout every province, was distributed to all the peoples so the Jews could be ready to avenge themselves against their enemies on that day. The couriers rode out in haste on *their royal horses at the king's urgent command. The law was also issued in the fortress of Susa. Mordecai went from the king's presence clothed in royal purple and white, with a great gold crown and a purple robe of fine linen. The city of Susa shouted and rejoiced, and the Jews celebrated with gladness, joy, and honor. In every province and every city, wherever the king's command and his law reached, joy and rejoicing took place among the Jews. There was a celebration and a holiday. And many of the ethnic groups of the land professed themselves to be Jews because fear of the Jews had overcome them" (Esther 8 HSCB).*

Chapter 9 - "Slaughtered"
Esther 9

PUT AN END TO THE ATTACKERS

So much time has passed. I have stayed busy writing about King Ahasuerus and all of the events that have unfolded over this period of time. Today is the day that the Jews were to be eradicated and completely annihilated. The thirteenth day of the twelfth month. Mordecai has exercised tremendous power in the palace, and he has become quite prominent throughout the provinces of Persia.

The Jews had gathered together in each province and city. Their attackers arrived ready to win and wipe out the Jews.
As they arrived, the Jews held their ground and they could not be overcome. In the city of Susa, over 500 people were slaughtered by the Jews. Haman's sons, all 10 of them were also killed on this day.

In an extraordinary turn of events, the king asked how many people had been executed. They reported the number to him, and he related it to Esther. At that time he asked, "What has been done in the rest of the royal provinces? Whatever your request it will be given to you. Esther answers, "If it delights you, O King, may the Jews in Susa carry out tomorrow the law of today. And may the 10 sons of Haman be lynched on the gallows?"
So the king gave an order for this to be done.

PURIM FEASTS ESTABLISHED-BANQUETS #9 AND #10

The Jews had been delivered from their enemies by annihilating them. On the thirteenth and fourteenth day they were executing many people, it was a bloodbath. On the fifteenth day, they rested with joy and feasting. On this fifteenth day, they made it their holiday called Purim. It is a holiday where they deliver gifts to each other. Mordecai recorded everything that had happened on the thirteenth, fourteenth, and fifteenth day. Queen Esther and Mordecai confirmed that the fourteenth and fifteenth day of the twelfth month would be the feast of Purim, to celebrate their escape from utter annihilation. The word Purim is taken from the word Pur, the lot that Haman had cast to pick the day to destroy and crush the Jews.

POINTS TO CONSIDER

#1-FINISH LINE/NO SUSPENSE

In the middle of the book of Esther, we find the promises of God threatened. Throughout the book, we never read or hear of His name. Therefore, we might wonder, like they might have wondered. Where is God? We find most of the tension in the earlier part of the book. Therefore, in the book we have drama and tension. Chapters three, four, and five all end with a cliffhanger. But then everything changes. Now, the enemies of the Jews have waited, plotting their attack. The Jews have had all this time to develop their defense. But as soon as we get to this chapter, there is no suspense and no drama. We would expect to read more drama and more suspense but instead, in the first verse, it is over. We know the finality of how it ends. It is comparatively like knowing the score of a football game before you get to watch the game. Why is there no suspense? Why does it become final in the first verse? It goes back to what Mordecai said in Chapter 4, verse 14. Many consider verse 14 of chapter 4 the key verse to the book of Esther, and this seems to hold true. Mordecai knew the answer back then when he said, *"If you keep silent at this time, relief and deliverance will arise for the Jews from another place....And who knows whether you have not come to the kingdom for such a time as this?"* Mordecai knew the ending, he knew the outcome. There was no suspense about whether or not God's people would be delivered. If you or I could have asked Mordecai how his people would have been delivered, his answer would have likely been, "I don't know!" But one thing he knew for sure, God would deliver His people.

#2-FEAST OF PURIM/ESTABLISHED

Esther's story ends by illustrating that when God seems silent, the best way to thrive is to celebrate the few ways in which he is clearly present. This is why the feast of Purim was established. There are some key factors that we need to look at when looking at this feast.

1. This party of Purim would remain a lasting practice, retained throughout every generation. This party was given for the work of God that was undeniable.
2. The party of Purim is referred to six times in Chapter 9. The word "confirm" or "obligate" is used. Two times, it says, "confirm" Purim through the writing of a letter. Four times it uses the word "obligate." These words do not refer to a person imposing their will upon another, instead it refers to the confirmation of a decision that was already made. This is a joyful celebration of God working behind the scenes.

3. The party of Purim is different than the other five feasts in the Torah. The other feasts were commanded by God and Moses. This feast is a natural response, a spontaneous response of Esther and the people to the work of God.
4. The party of Purim was named after the lot that was cast by Haman (PUR). The name is to remind God's people of how a great reversal came about. The feast of Purim is designed as a holiday to allow God's people to hope in their bleakest days.

PERSONAL APPLICATIONS

POA #1-WHERE we live

Once again, I am writing this chapter in a time when things all around us seem to have gone haywire. A black man has been murdered by a white police officer. Protests have ensued. Some protests have turned into riots. Buildings have been set on fire, police officers have been shot and killed. Others have been wounded in the chaos. Many of us might be asking, "Where is God?" We live in a broken world, and at times we find it difficult to see what God is doing. We want to believe that God is good, yet we look around and see all these bad things happening, believing the world is bad. We read God is love, yet we watch as the world seems full of hate. We hold onto the fact that God is in control, yet, we look around and see chaos. We read a Bible full of great promises, yet in our lives, we find disappointment and heartache. So many people think like this: "If God is in control, He isn't running the universe the way I would."

POA #2 - WE don't always understand

Frequently our lives are filled with drama. Our lives are like the middle of the book of Esther where circumstances can be altered instantly. One moment we are on the top of the world and the next moment it seems as though everything is coming apart at the seams.

A pastor friend of mine had left his church in Maine and moved to pastor a church in Nebraska. Not too long after arriving in Nebraska, his wife was in a horrible car accident which damaged her mind quite extensively. She had become a danger to herself and to others so they had to place her in a nursing home.

A young lady who lives in California had wed the man of her dreams. Their life seemed to be going so well. One day, he was helping a neighbor repair a motorcycle. When it was fixed, her husband decided to test it to see if it was running efficiently. When he took off, a dog ran in front of him, causing the cycle to flip forward, flinging him off. He hit his head on the ground and died there in the yard.

A young man who was headed for the ministry was excited for his mom to see him reach his dream. She had suffered from cancer for quite some time, and at times it seemed as though she was going to overcome it. But before she could see her son reach his dream, cancer overtook her body and she passed away.

Life is full of uncertainties, suspense, and drama. Things can change in a moment's notice. Off and on, life is scary, we don't know what the following steps will be. We don't always understand what happens at a certain moment. But there is one thing we can know for sure is we have a God that we can hold on to.

It is true for all of us that the middle of our story can go a number of possible ways. In the middle of our story, there are times when it seems the enemies of God will win. In the middle of our story, we will watch as the people of God suffer. In the middle of our story, someone might inquire of us if God is keeping His promises to us and the only answer we can come up with is, "I don't know."

We don't always understand what God is doing. We don't always comprehend why certain things happen in the middle of our story. But by reading the story of Esther we can know there is no suspense of how our story will end. When our paths seem unsure, the end will always be the same. In the end, God will always deliver His people. In the end, God will always deliver us. We can always know for sure that God will take care of His own.

POA #3-WE can live in a modern-day Purim

The party of Purim will help us cultivate a habit of celebration. It can help us realize that God is not hidden from us. He is not away on some vacation with His cell phone turned off. There are times when we can become disenchanted about God.

Ann Voskamp, the author of the book, "One Thousand Gifts," tells the tragic tale of her sister's death. Ann remembers how death rippled through her and her parent's lives. She became bitter and uneasy with God. Eventually, Ann found her way back to life with God. How? She practiced CELEBRATION. She read scripture over and over, realizing the fundamental call for our lives is celebration. At times, she still grieved the loss of her sister, but she intentionally sought reasons to rejoice. She knew that if she did this, she could find light and life again. She was determined to identify one thousand gifts given to her by God, even though she had lost her sister. She began by writing a journal keeping track of even the smallest gift she received from God each day. Her journal included the sound of pages turning, boys humming hymns, wind rushing through an open truck window, or laundry flapping in the wind. She ultimately found that by actively seeking God in these gifts and celebrating them she experienced transformation. [14]

Imagine if you and I would take the time each week to write down some things that we are grateful for. Maybe we could write down ten the first week, gradually moving up to one hundred per week. But not writing down obvious things like family or friends or Jesus. But to write down things that we often forget about like warm chocolate chip cookies, a dog wagging his tail or the feel of brand-new socks. Believe it or not, these too, are gifts from God. We could subsequently learn we can practice our own party of Purim by celebrating these things each week.

"The king's command and law went into effect on the thirteenth day of the twelfth month, the month Adar.On the day when the Jews' enemies had hoped to overpower them, just the opposite happened. The Jews overpowered those who hated them. In each of King Ahasuerus's provinces the Jews assembled in their cities to attack those who intended to harm them. Not a single person could withstand them; terror of them fell on every nationality. All the officials of the provinces, the satraps, the governors, and the royal civil administrators aided the Jews because they were afraid of Mordecai. For Mordecai exercised great power in the palace, and his fame spread throughout the provinces as he became more and more powerful. The Jews put all their enemies to the sword, killing and destroying them. They did what they pleased to those

who hated them. In the fortress of Susa the Jews killed and destroyed 500 men, including Parshandatha, Dalphon, Aspatha, Poratha, Adalia, Aridatha, Parmashta, Arisai, Aridai, and Vaizatha. They killed these 10 sons of Haman son of Hammedatha, the enemy of the Jews. However, they did not seize any plunder.

On that day the number of people killed in the fortress of Susa was reported to the king. The king said to Queen Esther, 'In the fortress of Susa the Jews have killed and destroyed 500 men, including Haman's 10 sons. What have they done in the rest of the royal provinces? Whatever you ask will be given to you. Whatever you seek will also be done.'

Esther answered, 'If it pleases the king, may the Jews who are in Susa also have tomorrow to carry out today's law, and may the bodies of Haman's 10 sons be hung on the gallows.' The king gave the orders for this to be done, so a law was announced in Susa, and they hung the bodies of Haman's 10 sons. The Jews in Susa assembled again on the fourteenth day of the month of Adar and killed 300 men in Susa, but they did not seize any plunder.The rest of the Jews in the royal provinces assembled, defended themselves, and got rid of their enemies. They killed 75,000 of those who hated them, but they did not seize any plunder. They fought on the thirteenth day of the month of Adar and rested on the fourteenth, and it became a day of feasting and rejoicing.But the Jews in Susa had assembled on the thirteenth and the fourteenth days of the month. They rested on the fifteenth day of the month, and it became a day of feasting and rejoicing. This explains why the rural Jews who live in villages observe the fourteenth day of the month of Adar as a time of rejoicing and feasting. It is a holiday when they send gifts to one another.

Mordecai recorded these events and sent letters to all the Jews in all of King Ahasuerus's provinces, both near and far. He ordered them to celebrate the fourteenth and fifteenth days of the month Adar every year because during those days the Jews got rid of their enemies. That was the month when their sorrow was turned into rejoicing and their mourning into a holiday. They were to be days of feasting, rejoicing, and of sending gifts to one another and the poor. So the Jews agreed to continue the practice they had begun, as Mordecai had written them to do. For Haman son of Hammedatha the Agagite, the enemy of all the Jews, had plotted against the Jews to destroy them. He cast the Pur (that is, the lot) to crush and destroy them. But when the matter was brought before the king, he commanded by letter that the evil plan Haman had devised against the Jews return on his own head and that he should be hanged with his sons on the gallows. For this reason these days are called Purim, from the word Pur. Because of all the instructions in this letter as well as what they had witnessed and what had happened to them, the Jews bound themselves, their descendants, and all who joined with them to a commitment that they would not fail to celebrate these two days each and every year according to the written instructions and according to the time appointed. These days are remembered and celebrated by every generation, family, province, and city, so that these days of Purim will not lose their significance in Jewish life and their memory will not fade from their descendants.Queen Esther daughter of Abihail, along with Mordecai the Jew, wrote this second letter with full authority to confirm the letter about Purim. He sent letters with messages of peace and faithfulness to all the Jews who were in the 127 provinces of the kingdom of

Ahasuerus, in order to confirm these days of Purim at their proper time just as Mordecai the Jew and Queen Esther had established them and just as they had committed themselves and their descendants to the practices of fasting and lamentation. So Esther's command confirmed these customs of Purim, which were then written into the record" (Esther 9 HCSB).

Chapter 10 - "Honored"
Esther 10

POWER AND POSITION OF MORDECAI

It has been a wonderful time living in the capital city of Persia for a number of years now. Watching the scenes unfold, listening to the stories of those in the palace. Before I prepare to make my way out of here, I stop by to see the king. I wish him well. I stop by to see Queen Esther. I talk with her for awhile letting her know that she will be mentioned as one of the greatest women I have known. But then I make my way over to Mordecai, he is right now the second most powerful person in the kingdom. He informed me that everything that he has done is now recorded in the history books titled, "Kings of Media and Persia." Mordecai knew he was powerful, he knew he was popular. He said, " I will continue to do good for my people. I will speak for the welfare of all my descendants." At that time he shook my hand and said, "Thanks for writing all these things down. But most of all, "When God seems hidden, trust in Him because He is consistently working for His people."

I turned to walk out of the palace. My notes in my hand. I can't wait to get back to my home, so I can put together my book. I am elated I accepted the invitation the king had sent to me. It has been a thrilling time. I walk down the street, hop on the connecting bus, ready and willing to embark on another adventure if I am invited.

POINT TO BE CONSIDERED/PERSONAL APPLICATION

HOPE

I combined these two for the concluding chapter because there is one thing I desire to talk about. That one thing is the word, HOPE!

As we have already noticed the Persian empire was massive, the power they possessed was monumental. But when the book of Esther closes, we do not see the world of the excesses of which we read about in the beginning but we see how far Mordecai has come. Mordecai was loyal to the king and to his people. In the book of Esther, we watch as two of God's people are elevated to great positions. Esther, an orphan, being raised by her cousin, is now queen of one of the greatest empires. Mordecai, a humble servant of God, gave of himself in every possible way is currently able to dramatically influence the world around him for good.

What do we discover in the final chapter of Esther? HOPE! We are foreigners in a strange land. Our Christian life can be difficult as we traverse through this world. I know some who are ready to get out of this wicked world, longing for the shores of heaven. Waiting for God to come and take His children home. I know the Bible instructs us to be watchful for that day. But if we are only thinking of the next life, then we are missing out on some incredible and beautiful things in this life.

One thing the book of Esther teaches us is that God has a purpose for placing us in this world. We were created to live a life that would impact others, reshape history, and fill this earth with good works so that others might benefit.

Before I close out this book, I pray that the book and story of Esther will influence us. I pray today that we will live life with the courage of Esther and the wisdom of Mordecai. I pray that you will believe just as Mordecai believed, "You are here for such a time as this." There is a reason you are here, there is a reason that God has called you, there is a reason why you have chosen to read this book. There is hope for each of us for we have been chosen by God, for His glory.

CONCLUSION

One of the most incredible stories ever written was the book of Esther. For in it holds excitement, suspense, drama, irony, and truth. Esther is seen as a history book, but it is more than that, it is a tremendous story that demonstrates how God preserves His people. It is a remarkable story that proves God keeps His promises. Even though throughout the story God seems hidden, He is working behind the scenes orchestrating some exceptional and unbelievable events in order to preserve His people. The story of Esther is reassurance for us when God seems distant or absent from our lives.

God's people are living in a foreign land, surrounded by people who do not share their same view of God. They are hemmed in by a society that looks at outward appearances, trying to persuade them to enjoy the amusements of this world. Sounds much like the world in which we live, doesn't it?

In the book of Esther, we saw self-indulgence of a king, hate, and pride from one man who puts out a "hit" on the people of God. They were facing danger and extinction. Yet, throughout the pages, God seemed to not be there. He seemed to be hiding in the darkness.

The TRUTH is: In Esther, God was so inconspicuous His name is never mentioned. Moreover, God has been more dominant than we realized. When you expand the story of Esther, it seems that God operated more in the darkness than He did in the spotlight. There were times when God's presence is extremely difficult to recognize and His plan was hard to conceive. Godless people were crusading to conduct God's business. It was a time when the blaze of hope had been smothered by the ashes of suffering and a time when God's identity was hard to discover, yet all the while He was in operation.

The FACT is: When God seems as if He has dropped out of sight, He is here in this present moment. When God seems as though He has fallen asleep, He is awake and active. When God seems hidden, He is visible. The book of Esther shows us we are not meant to live woefully or with worry, but we are to live for adventurous festivities.

The book of Esther is a splendid story. Chris Altrock, the author of the book, "Behind Esther: Thriving When God Seems Distant" says, *"A story that, on the surface appears to be Godless but, upon further examination, is God-full."*[15]

Karen Jobes says, *"The book of Esther is perhaps the most striking biblical statement of what systematic theologians call the providence of God. When we speak of God's providence, we mean that God, in some invisible and inscrutable way, governs all creatures, actions, and circumstances through the normal and the ordinary course of human life, without the intervention of the miraculous. The book of Esther is the most true to life biblical examples of God's providence precisely because God seems absent."* [16]

At long last, I want to say that if you find yourself living in a time, season, or space when it is hard to find God because things seem routine or filled with suffering, then trust that God is present and active in your life. Give thanks to God. Don't yearn for a different story. Give thanks to God for your Esther story.

When God seems *hugely hidden*, He is *astonishingly available*. When God seems *sorely stagnant*, He is *wondrously working*. You might have to undertake some extensive investigative work. You might be unable to just sit back and wait for God to appear. You might have to get up, get out, and dissect through each event of each day or week. But do not fear. God is there. The evidence is there. The proof of God being with you, being there is all around, we merely have to look.

This is the story of the gospel. Jesus seemed to be on a path that would cause death, mourning and sadness. He was on a collision course with the cross. The torment of the crucifixion was headed His way. But God already had a plan in place. Resurrection! A plan that would lead to joy, happiness, and celebration. At the end of three days, the stone that sealed the tomb would roll away.

King David grasped this. He endured his reasonable share of heartache. But at the same time, He knew God would bring joy in the midst of his pain. He knew that God would reverse his mourning and turn it into dancing. In fact, he composed a song about it. The significant reversal was Esther's song. It can also be our song. No matter what you are going through today, there is a reverse and it is possible.

Mordecai knew God was working behind the scenes. Esther mustered the courage to go before the king. Neither of these individuals just sat back and allowed things to happen. They stood up, they got their hands dirty. They made sure they participated for God. They stood in the middle of an ungodly place, with ungodly people, all the while trusting in God, even when He seemed to be nowhere in sight.

I challenge each one of us today, no matter what our circumstances are, to move to the center of the arena. When life seems to be crumbling around us, when our plans have to change or our dreams start to fade, let's trust in God, even when He seems hidden.

An author Brene Brown says this, "It's not the critic who counts. Not the man who points out how the strong man stumbles, or where the doer of deeds could have done them better. The credit belongs to the man who is actually in the arena, whose face is marred by sweat and dust and blood; who strives valiantly;...who at the best knows in the end the triumph of high achievement, and who at the worst, if he fails, at least fails while daring greatly." [17]

SUMMARY AND INTERSTING FACTS

In the book of Esther there are no clues given to help us determine the identity of who the author is. Some believe it could possibly be Ezra or Nehemiah. There are also some who believe it could be Mordecai, or possibly a close associate of his. The unknown author was probably a Jew who was familiar with the royal Persian court, as well as an eyewitness to all the events that occurred in the book.

The book was for the principle character of the the story, the star of the story, Esther. Her name means "star." Her Hebrew name was "Hadassah" and she was taken from her home. She was adopted and brought up by her cousin Mordecai.

Also, we do not get a clear picture of when the book was written. Even though many believe the events were between 486 BC to 465 BC, during the reign of King Xerxes (Ahasueres). Some believe the book was written somewhere around 460 BC.

During this time period, many Jews had returned to Judah, but Esther, Mordecai, along with many other Jews, were content to stay in Susa, the capital city of Persia.

The purpose of the book of Esther was to record the history of the Feast of Purim, the Jewish persecution, as well as their protection. The providence of God is evident in the book of Esther, even though the name of God is never mentioned. Also, the word prayer or worship is never seen. One reason for this is because they were under the Persian dictatorship, which would not allow the mention of these things. Even though there is no mention of God, we can see His hand, providence, power, protection, and His grace throughout the book.

There are some key points in the book of Esther which include two major plots, two heroes three cliffhangers, seven roads with a u-turn, and ten banquets.

TWO MAJOR PLOTS

1. A young Jewish girl is carried away into the harem of an arrogant, womanizing, power-loving, unsteady, volatile, savage king.

2. An egotistical, hate-filled man, Haman, gets elevated to the second most powerful position in Persia.

THREE HEROES

1. Esther is presented as the hero, taken away from her home, later she becomes the queen. She uses her wit and grit to save an entire nation.

2. Mordecai doesn't seem like the hero. From the start to the ending he just goes to work, doing his job. It's not flashy, it's often forgettable, but God uses him going to work and he ends up saving a nation.

3. God is the true hero in the book of Esther.

THREE CLIFFHANGERS

1. The capital city, Susa, is completely disoriented because of the king's decree to destroy all Jews-End of Chapter 3.

2. Esther consents to go before the king, risking her life in the process. Her final message to Mordecai is, "If I perish, I perish."-End of Chapter 4

3. When Esther stands before the king, he asks her what her request is, she invites the king to a meal she is preparing for him and Haman. As suspense builds he tries to find out what she wants at the meal, she

doesn't tell him, she puts it off for one more day.-Chapter 5

SEVEN ROADS WITH A U-TURN

1. The signet ring is given to Haman, who writes a decree to kill the Jews. Esther 3:10. **U-TURN:** The signet ring is given to Mordecai, who writes a decree to save the Jews. Esther 8:2

2. Haman is promoted, he is given charge of all the Jews and their properties. Esther 3:11 **U-TURN:** Mordecai is promoted, he is given all of Haman's property. Esther 8:2

3. Letters are sent to every province decreeing that all Jews will be attacked and annihilated. Esther 3:13 **U-TURN:** Letters are sent to every province decreeing that the Jews can defend themselves and annihilated the people. Esther 8:11

4. Mordecai is humble, therefore, he dresses in sackcloth and ashes. Esther 4:11 **U-TURN:** Mordecai is honored, therefore, he dresses in royal clothing. Esther 8:15

5. Haman builds a gallows to hang Mordecai. Esther 5:14 **U-TURN:** Haman gets hung on the gallows intended for Mordecai. Esther 7:10

6. Haman believes the king is going to honor him with a royal robe and a public parade. Esther 6:7 **U-TURN:** The king honors Mordecai with a royal robe and a public parade. Esther 6:11

7. Esther 4:3 says, "There was great mourning among the Jewish people in every province where the king's command and edict came. They fasted, wept, and lamented, and many lay on sackcloth and ashes." **U-TURN:** Esther 8:17 says, "In every province and every city, wherever the king's command and his law reached, joy and rejoicing took place among the Jews. There was a celebration and a holiday."

TEN BANQUETS

1. 180 day banquet for all nobles. Esther 1:2-4
2. 7 day banquet for all men. Esther 1:5-8
3. Queen Vashti's banquet for all women. Esther 1:9
4. A banquet for Esther, the new queen. Esther 2:18
5. The king and Haman's banquet for the new decree.
   Esther 3:15
6. Esther's first banquet for the king and Haman. Esther 5:5-8
7. Esther's second banquet pointing the finger at Haman. Esther 7:1-9
8. A public banquet honoring Mordecai. Esther 8:17
9. The Jewish victory banquet in all provinces. Esther 9:17
10. A Jewish victory banquet in Susa. Esther 9:18

Notes

1. James Strong, The New Strong's Exhaustive Concordance, 1995-1996, Nashville, Tennessee, Thomas Nelson Publishers
2. Ian Duguid, Esther and Ruth, 2005, Phillipsburg: P&R Publishing, 27
3. Elayne A. Saltzberg, Joan C. Chrisler, "Beauty is the Beast: Psychological Effects of the Pursuit of the Perfect Female Body," 1995, Mountain View, California, Mayfield Publishing Company, "Women: A Feminist Perspective, 306-315
4. https://www.dictionary.com/browse/fear
5. Timothy Caine, "The God of Great Reversals," 2016, United States of America
6. C.S. Lewis, "The Screwtape Letters," 2003, Paperback Edition
7. Tim Keller, "The Man The King Delights To Honor," 2007, Sermon
8. Chris Altrock, "Behind Esther, Thriving When God Seems Distant", 2019, Abilene, Texas, Leafwood Publishers
9. "We Bought A Zoo", Youtube, https://www.youtube.com/watch?V=ZmMFIganRQY
10. Jonathan Edwards, "Charity and Its Fruits", 2000, Carlisle, Pennsylvania, "The Banner of Truth"
11. National Fire Protection Association, https://www.nfpa.org/News-and-Research/Data-research-and-tools/Emergency-Responders/Firefighter-fatalities-in-the-United-States/Firefighter-deaths, 6/5/2020
12. USA Today News, https://www.usatoday.com/story/news/2018/12/27/police-deaths-144-killed-line-duty-2018, 6/5/2020
13. Wikipedia, https://en.wikipedia.org/wiki/Emergency_workers_killed_in_the_September_11_attacks, 6/3/2020
14. Ann Voscamp, "One Thousand Gifts: A Dare To Live Fully Right Where You Are", 2010, Grand Rapids, Michigan, Zondervan Publishing
15. Chris Altrock, "Behind Esther, Thriving When God Seems Distant", 2019, Abilene, Texas, Leafwood Publishers, 14

16. Karen Jobes, "Esther, The NIV Application Commentary, 1999, Grand Rapids, Michigan, Zondervan Publishing, 19-20, 43

17. Brene Brown, "Rising Strong", 2017, New York, Random House Publishing, 20-21

Printed in Great Britain
by Amazon